PRAISE FOR
FELICE DOUGLAS AND
COLLEGE MOMENTUM ACADEMY

"Through her personal college experiences, Felice was able to relate to our daughter in a positive way. She didn't rush our daughter through the door but took her time to answer every question with no time restraints. As a result, we are 100 percent satisfied with Felice's services and highly recommend her to anyone looking to enter college."

—THE EDMONDS FAMILY

"I am happy to share that our daughter was accepted into six of the seven schools that she applied to. Fortunately, she still has great options to choose from.

We thank Felice for the guidance she provided through the essay writing process. We believe that it was the key to her success. We've seen many of our daughter's peers with outstanding grades and resumes not experience the same success."

—THE GRAY FAMILY

"I have always described Felice to others as my 'angel in disguise.' She served as a source of inspiration for me—a light at the end of the tunnel, so to speak. Not only did she guide us through all the frightening overload of financial aid paperwork but she did this with the biggest smile on her face. No matter the day or the time, Felice was always there to lend a helping hand when it came to understanding the overall college admissions process.

It is rare to find people like Felice who care so much and have so much passion for their line of work. I am both honored and proud to call her not only my financial aid counselor but also a true and dear friend."

—THE PEREZ FAMILY

"Felice guided my daughter through the entire application process and how to make her essays robust, with not only attention to detail but also cognizant of submission deadlines. We appreciated her help every step of the way and recommend her as a superb college and career coach to anyone heading to college."

—THE KHAN FAMILY

"Felice was there to support, comfort, encourage, and guide us with any question or concern that we had. Her friendly and approachable manner allowed us to work together and understand the process of financial aid. Paying for college can be a very confusing process, but it was always comforting to know we had a great college counselor there. She guided us to potential scholarships and was a support system when we received one."

—TIFFANY, STUDENT

"Thank you for allowing us to experience the best four years of our lives and for being there as we venture out to our next journey! We've learned so much academically and even more of who we are, about others, and the beauty of making a change. Thank you for making a difference. We know you will strive to do the same for others!"

—STEPHANIE, STUDENT

HOW TO GET YOUR
CHILD INTO
COLLEGE

HOW TO GET YOUR
CHILD INTO
COLLEGE

THE PARENTS' GUIDE TO
COLLEGE PLANNING

FELICE DOUGLAS

Advantage®

Published by Advantage, Charleston, South Carolina.
Member of Advantage Media Group.

ADVANTAGE is a registered trademark, and the Advantage colophon is a trademark of Advantage Media Group, Inc.

Printed in the United States of America.

10 9 8 7 6 5 4 3 2 1

ISBN: 978-1-59932-497-5
LCCN: 2017940138

Cover design by George Stevens.
Layout design by Megan Elger.

This publication is designed to provide accurate and authoritative information in regard to the subject matter covered. It is sold with the understanding that the publisher is not engaged in rendering legal, accounting, or other professional services. If legal advice or other expert assistance is required, the services of a competent professional person should be sought.

Advantage Media Group is proud to be a part of the Tree Neutral® program. Tree Neutral offsets the number of trees consumed in the production and printing of this book by taking proactive steps such as planting trees in direct proportion to the number of trees used to print books. To learn more about Tree Neutral, please visit **www.treeneutral.com.**

Advantage Media Group is a publisher of business, self-improvement, and professional development books. We help entrepreneurs, business leaders, and professionals share their Stories, Passion, and Knowledge to help others Learn & Grow. Do you have a manuscript or book idea that you would like us to consider for publishing? Please visit **advantagefamily.com** or call **1.866.775.1696.**

To Alex, my favorite person. Ever.

TABLE OF CONTENTS

ACKNOWLEDGMENTS

I am extremely grateful for the opportunity to help students and families make their dreams come true through higher education.

To the fantastic team at Advantage: Thank you so much for your patience and encouragement. I am especially grateful to Scott Neville and Alex Rogers.

To my family: Mom, you have always provided unwavering support, and you are the best role model I could have asked for. Adam, Star, and Camia, I love you all. Dorothea, you have been my big sis and mentor throughout our four decades of best friendship. Tim, you are my rock. Thank you for always being on my side.

To my accountability partners: Jennifer Jessie, thank you for holding my feet to the fire daily. Nicole Chamblin and the Visionary Goal Getters, thank you for helping me push through to the end of this project.

To all of the students and families with whom I have had the privilege to work over the years: I am eternally grateful to you for allowing me to be part of your team.

INTRODUCTION

As parents, one of our greatest desires is to have each of our children get an excellent education and start life with a successful job and no debt.

But the reality is that the average student takes four and a half years to graduate with a bachelor's degree, therefore delaying the start of that exciting new life.[1] In addition, it typically takes new college graduates three to nine months to find a job, and then they end up leaving it within two years[2] with a debt of more than $30,000 hanging over their heads.[3]

The worst part is that newly minted college graduates are likely to move back in with their families. As of 2017, the average age of young persons leaving home for good is twenty-six.[4] That means they don't get married or start a family until they're thirty—at least. So it's taking longer than ever for students to make the transition from college to the real world, or they work while shouldering a mountain of student debt.

---

1   National Center for Education Statistics, Fast Facts, https://nces.ed.gov/fastfacts/display.asp?id=569

2   Experience, "Career Statistics," https://www.experience.com/alumnus/article?channel_id=career_management&source_page=additional_articles&article_id=article_1247505066959

3   The Institute for College Access and Success, Project on Student Debt, http://ticas.org/posd/map-state-data

4   Camila Domonoske, "For First Time in 130 Years, More Young Adults Live with Parents Than with Partners," National Public Radio, March 24, 2016, http://www.npr.org/sections/thetwo-way/2016/05/24/479327382/for-first-time-in-130-years-more-young-adults-live-with-parents-than-partners

As a parent, you may feel you haven't planned sufficiently early and haven't saved enough money. Or perhaps you haven't made it clear to your children that they must participate in the process. As a matter of fact, most of my students from middle-income families believe that their parents have enough money to pay for college out of pocket and that looking for scholarships isn't necessary. Your children may be saying, "My parents have it covered. We live a nice life. They have nice cars, and we have a great house, so I'm sure that they have the money to pay for college."

Many of the reasons for this disconnect are out of your control. College has changed since you were in high school. The admissions process has become much more cumbersome, requires higher levels of preparation, and seems to be much more competitive than in decades past. College also costs much more, as a percentage of household income.

The good news is that your family can do this! There is definitely a path to making your child's dreams happen, and that's why you have this extremely detailed book in hand. The action steps in these pages will help you guide your student to choose a career path and get into a college that is a good fit.

My strategies are tailored to families seeking an excellent education for their children without going into debt and without killing each other in the process and to parents who feel their students need to get a jump on college admissions because they have less-than-perfect grades or are not yet sure of what they want to study. I also hope this guide will be a valuable resource for students who have excelled in high school and want to put together an application package that will get them into a top-tier university.

These chapters include dozens of things you need to know to manage the college admissions process more easily and work smarter, not harder.

What you'll also find is that each section includes practical advice, concrete action steps, proven resources, and time-saving recommendations. This means you don't need to reinvent the wheel to help your child complete college applications. The tools are handed to you.

You may not agree with some of the advice I give, and that is okay. My hope is that it sparks discussion in your family and with other parents in your circle. There is no one-size-fits-all strategy for college admissions. Each family's journey is very personal.

MY GUIDING PRINCIPLES

Throughout the book, I will refer to the guiding principles that define college admissions success. You and your family are encouraged to develop your own. In the meantime, here are the guiding principles that direct me in my work with students and provide the framework for this guide.

- **The college admissions process works best when it is a family project.** Even though students must take primary responsibility for getting into college, they need parental support and guidance to help them through the experience.

- **Early planning is the key to avoiding stress and feeling overwhelmed.** It is absolutely critical that students make time before their senior year to plan for and execute the college admissions process.

- **There is no such thing as the one perfect college.** There are over four thousand traditional colleges and universities in the United States, from community colleges to the universities of the Ivy League. All students can find several colleges that will fit their needs.

- **College and career planning go hand in hand.** Students who make an effort to be exposed to hands-on career experiences while still in high school make more confident college choices.

- **Families should exhaust all possible ways of paying for college before using student loans.** Scholarships can make the difference between graduating debt-free and paying back tens of thousands of dollars over the next decade or more.

Everything in these pages points back to these beliefs. The one principle that does apply to every family is that waiting too long to take forward action can have unwanted consequences. It is always better to take action too early rather than too late. My wish for you is that no matter what grade your student is in now, you begin taking the steps outlined here so you keep gaining momentum.

STEP ONE

MAKE COLLEGE ADMISSIONS PLANNING A FAMILY PRIORITY

Ava was an excellent student. She was second in her class, had excellent test scores, and participated in a ton of activities such as student government and Model UN. She expected to get into any college she wanted.

Ava's parents expected her to apply to private colleges. They were confident that not only would she get several acceptances but she would also earn full scholarships, enabling them to afford the expense.

Overconfident, Ava only applied to three public colleges: a very competitive in-state university, a highly competitive out-of-state university, and her "safety" school (which she really wasn't interested in at all). She got into two schools but was wait-listed at her top choice.

Ava didn't understand that her parents didn't have the money to pay for college out of pocket. Her parents didn't know that Ava had applied only to three public universities.

The family had a major communications failure and ended up painting themselves into a corner.

What went wrong?

- **The family did not develop an application strategy.** Ava and her parents were not on the same page when it came to the list of potential schools and the need for scholarship aid. It was crucial that they talk this out as a family so that there were no surprises.

- **Ava did not apply to enough colleges.** There are no guarantees in college admissions, even for an excellent student like Ava, so she had to give herself several options. Every student should apply to a mix of colleges with various attributes: public, private, highly selective, and more inclusive.

- **Ava should not have applied to any college that she wasn't really interested in attending.** Ava didn't get off the waiting list for her top choice college. Her parents couldn't afford the out-of-state university, so she ended up attending her safety school. It was not a good fit, and her first year was very difficult.

Family communication and early planning would have given her a better chance at finding a college that was the right fit. Unfortunately, Ava's only choice was to attend her safety school.

One of the first things that you need to do to prepare for the college planning process is to make certain that you create *time* for college planning. Most students put the application process on the back burner and only start thinking about it when they're under the gun in their senior year. Early planning ensures that you and your student will have enough time to do it well.

HAVE A FAMILY MEETING

How can you be sure that everyone in your family—parents *and* students—is on the same page with college planning?

Having a quick chat in the car on the way home from soccer practice is not enough. Neither is just telling students to see their counselor. There has to be a meeting of the minds for everyone in the family, and the best way to do that is to plan a series of family discussions.

The first dialogue is just for the adults primarily responsible for paying for college.

Whether you're a parent who has been married for twenty-five years or you have been coparenting from separate homes since your child was two, it is imperative that you both sit down together and figure out where you agree and disagree on expectations for your student and the finances.

If you are a single or widowed parent raising your children on your own, I highly encourage you to have this meeting with an accountability partner—a trusted family member or friend with whom you feel comfortable discussing this, especially the financial issues. You might want to choose someone who has already sent children to college so that person can share some wisdom.

You will want to find answers to questions such as:

- Do you expect your student to attend a public college nearby or are you open to letting her go further away?

- Are you on board with your student's career choice?

- And most importantly, how much money have you set aside to pay for college?

This isn't a discussion of how much money you earn or how much you have in a retirement account. You are only to consider the amount you currently have saved and earmarked for college. Whether it is $200 or $200,000, you have to talk about it.

The next discussion, of course, is with your student. This is really where the rubber meets the road because you each are going to share your thoughts about college.

Yes, parents, you are going to allow your children to tell you all of their hopes and dreams, and you will simply listen and acknowledge. Share your hopes and dreams for them as well, and you've set the stage for the next part of the conversation: the money.

I am constantly reminding parents that college is a six-figure investment. Remember your teenagers have no idea how much money that really is. They may assume you're simply going to pay for everything or, conversely, you're unable to help at all.

Please tell your child the truth about your financial picture and reassure him or her that you will find a way to make it work, as a team effort.

I am encouraging you, no matter what grade your student is in right now, to plan your first couple of family discussions. You'll find that adding a little structure to this process will help with communication and get everyone in the family onto the same page.

CHOOSE YOUR ADVISORY TEAM

Do you know where most students get the bulk of their college admissions information? Other high school students. Talk about the blind leading the blind.

Parents are also getting the scoop from other parents who may or may not have sent students to college. While it is to your advantage to talk to people walking in your shoes, you cannot rely solely on their singular experiences. You have no idea if their children have grades, test scores, or interests that are comparable to those of your child. You also don't know their financial situation.

So, whom should you put on your advisory team?

School Counselors

Your best information will come from counselors and advisors who work with students. They have helped students to successfully apply to hundreds of colleges, and they've worked with others whose applications were declined.

Having the school counselor on your team may seem obvious, but I am always surprised by how many students and parents have not initiated direct contact with the school counselor by their senior year. Counselors are often extremely overloaded with students (four hundred or more in many public schools) and college planning is only one of their many responsibilities.

Families must be proactive. Don't wait until the counseling staff comes to you to start communicating. Introduce yourself at every school event. When calling or sending e-mail, please be patient, as it may take a day or two to reply.

Some high schools are fortunate enough to have dedicated college counselors (sometimes called career counselors or career center specialists). They certainly belong on your team as well.

Teachers

Your student's teachers are an invaluable resource for your family. Aside from the daily academic support they provide, teachers are very likely to be your student's most trusted advisors and mentors.

Many colleges require one or more letters of recommendation from your student's teachers. These letters are important because teachers can describe your student's strengths, accomplishments, and personality in a way that the transcript cannot. Your student may need to have several of these recommendations, so it is important to get his teachers on your team.

Also, remember that all of your child's teachers are college graduates, so they have experiences and insight to share. Encourage your student to ask teachers about where they attended college and why.

Grandparents and Extended Family

Many grandparents who have saved money that their grandchildren will eventually inherit may want to find ways to support their heirs now. So what can they give besides clothes and video games? The answer for most families, without a doubt, is more money for college.

The first step is to set up a college saving account for each grandchild. There are a ton of options for saving, including 529 college saving plans, Uniform Gift to Minors Act (UGMA) and Uniform Transfer to Minors Act (UTMA) accounts, and annuities. Consult an experienced financial advisor to find the best options.

What else can Grandpa and NaNa do now to support their future college students?

- **Pay for a summer program.** One of the best things a student can do while in high school is to spend part of a summer living on a college campus and taking classes taught by professors.

- **Hire an SAT tutor.** Help your student score higher on the Scholarship Aptitude Test (SAT) or American College Testing (ACT), which may lead to more choices in the college admissions process.

- **Take your student on a college tour.** Parents are often too busy with work to take their child out of town to see colleges, but a college tour gives retired grandparents a chance to steal their grandchildren away for a few days.

How can grandparents decide which activities to fund? A friend of mine whose family is from Ghana told me that her family uses a panel of aunts. The aunts and grandmothers pool resources to educate the children. All young persons must make a presentation to the panel, outlining their educational plans, and ask the panel for the funds. After much cross-examination, the panel approves or sends the student back to make revisions. Talk about preparing the student for the real world!

Friends and Neighbors

Your family friends and neighbors have watched your son or daughter grow up, and they may be willing to be of service if asked. Choose those that have sent children to college within the last ten years because college admissions and financial aid have changed dramatically in the last decade or so. Talk to them about their experiences as a whole and in graphic detail—the good, the bad, and the ugly.

TIP:

Take their advice with a grain of salt—everyone has different wants and needs—and what they were looking for in a college or financial aid package may not reflect your family's goals. They also may not be completely forthcoming about certain specifics such as their students' grades or the family finances.

Youth Leaders

Your child's other influencers include scout leaders, youth pastors, job supervisors, music teachers, and sports coaches. All of these adults have insight into your student's personality. They all have experiences that your student can learn from.

HELP YOUR STUDENT WITH TIME MANAGEMENT

Many of the students with whom I work are seriously pressed for time. Between advanced classes, extracurricular activities, volunteering, and a part-time job, there doesn't seem to be enough time to relax, let alone get enough sleep.

One of the first things we do in our work together is what I call a time audit. We write down everything the students do every day for seven days in a row.

We account for every moment—time spent getting ready in the morning, in class, doing after-school activities, studying—everything. This process can really give you and your student a more realistic view of what is really taking up precious time.

For example, it may seem as if your student spends four hours a night doing homework, but in reality, she takes two thirty-minute breaks to talk on the phone. So homework only took three hours.

Or maybe your student plans to go to bed at ten but regularly stays up past midnight. Tracking bedtime is especially crucial since studies show that teens and young adults perform better with about nine hours of sleep per night.[5]

Try it out with your teenager. For the next seven days, keep an accurate log of your student's daily activities. Write down everything including socializing and sleeping. This is for your student's benefit,

---

5   Mary A. Carskadon, "Sleep and Teens – Biology and Behavior," National Sleep Foundation, https://sleepfoundation.org/ask-the-expert/sleep-and-teens-biology-and-behavior.

so be truthful. Later, we'll discuss how to strategically use time more wisely so that your student has more time to relax, socialize, and, most importantly, get enough sleep.

I have some suggestions for making sure that students stay focused on a task until it gets done. These strategies make them feel better about getting things done in a timely manner, and they may be able to get an extra twenty minutes here and thirty minutes there throughout the day.

- **Set a deadline.** The first one—and this is the one I use most often and has benefitted me the most—is setting a definite end time. For example, I may decide at the beginning of the day that no matter what, I am going to stop working at six. So I'd better hurry up and get this done because I'm not working past that time. That end time for your student might be eight or ten, but find what works.

- **Timer method.** The timer method is for students who work better in spurts. Have your student set a timer for twenty minutes and work hard for that short burst. She should then take a five- or ten-minute break to answer messages and get some water before setting the timer for another twenty minutes of uninterrupted work. Doing that helps students avoid fatigue. They can stand up and walk around to get the blood flowing again before jumping back in and working a little bit harder.

- **Turn off all alerts.** Another thing students absolutely have to do is turn off the alerts on their phones and computers. It is really difficult to get back on track once focus has been disrupted. That phone/computer message is not important right now; schoolwork is. So turn off the alerts. All of those messages will be there at break time.

- **Give it away.** Another thing students may have to do if they just cannot resist the phone is give it to somebody to keep for them. If your student is working at home, you can hold on to the phone until it is time for a formal break. That way your student won't be distracted by it.

- **Keep your eyes on your student.** The last thing— and one that I still use sometimes—is being where you can watch your student. Students often stay more focused when they have another set of eyes on them. This will work well if your student is happy to share the same room with you. If that's just too much, your student can try working at the library or a spot such as Panera (which, for me, feels like my second office). The other people there may not present a distraction—and your student cannot watch TV!

Find one or more of those strategies that will work to help your student stay focused, which will allow more time later for other things your student wants to do.

FINDING THE TIME FOR COLLEGE PLANNING

Logan was a busy high school student. Between his heavy Advanced Placement (AP) course load, track practice, SAT tutoring, and an active social life, he felt stressed and overwhelmed. He thought there was no way he could find an additional two hours per week to plan for college.

The first step in our work together was to conduct a time audit. We accounted for every moment of his day for one full week. We wrote down the time he got up in the morning, how long it took for him to get ready for school, what time track practice ended, and how many hours he spent doing homework. We even tracked his personal time on the weekends.

It turns out that Logan got up at 6 a.m. and went to bed after midnight. He had track meets every Saturday and slept until noon on Sunday.

Logan was completely burned out. He worked four hours per night on homework but still managed to spend time with his friends. When I asked him about his work habits, I found that he was doing what most of us unsuccessfully try to do: multitasking. Logan was absolutely sure that he worked better when he was distracted by the phone.

I challenged Logan to try the timer method when doing his homework for one week. He started working at 6 p.m. and continued until 6:20 p.m. He took a break until 6:30 p.m. and then worked undistracted until 6:50 p.m. He continued working in twenty-minute spurts until 10 p.m., when he had to stop for the night. No more working until midnight.

Using the timer method forced Logan to prioritize his assignments in a new way since he had less time in which to complete them. He also had to train his friends to understand that there were times when he was unavailable.

He started getting to bed by 11 p.m. every night. He felt more rested and would go to school focused and less rushed. Since he didn't need to sleep until noon on Sunday, he could more easily find the two hours he needed to focus solely on college planning. He spent Sundays completing college applications and refining his essays. This schedule left him ready to jump back into schoolwork on Sunday evening to prepare for the new school week.

Logan posted his new schedule in his room and stuck to it for the rest of the semester. He managed to keep up his excellent grades and get his college applications done without becoming stressed out or losing any sleep.

Everything gets done only when there is a schedule to adhere to. This can't be done haphazardly, since there is so much to get accomplished.

Two hours per week is the minimum amount of time that a high school junior or senior can expect to spend on college applications, scholarship applications, and career research. It is best to get into the habit as early as possible.

Hold this time sacred and add it to the family calendar. Treat it as you would any other obligation. If your family has an activity that interferes with college planning time, don't cancel it. Simply move it to another time during the same week. This time is important, so handle it as such.

SUCCESS IS ...

Is success earning a degree? Landing the perfect job? Making a huge amount of money?

Over time, our definition of success can change, and it can really be a moving target for our young people. What can students do to define success for themselves?

- **Make a success wall.** Looking at ideas of success first thing in the morning and last thing at night can really cement those ideas in a young person's mind. Students can choose a wall of their bedroom to designate as a place for inspiration. They can print their ideas of success on large cards and post them where they can see them every day.

- **Create a vision board.** A vision board represents a student's biggest dreams and aspirations. Encourage your teenager to create a poster collage of her plans for the future. She will need poster board, magazines, and other decorating materials to make a project that is a reflection of whom she is now and whom she plans to be.

- **Put together a portfolio.** A portfolio is a collection of information, designed to help students tell their story when applying for college admission and scholarships. We will go into detail about this in step two.

Encourage your student to use one, two, or all three of these tools to reinforce ideas of success and to keep the focus on what can be done now to move in that direction.

The secret to a smooth transition from high school to college is making the admissions process a priority for the entire family. Before making any other decisions, sit down and define your family's guiding principles, supporting players, and winning outcomes together.

ACTION STEPS

❯ Have the first family discussion. Schedule a date and time for each subsequent meeting and stick to the plan.

❯ Help your student make a list of supporters by name. What can they contribute to the team? Contact each person and ask for support. This is a great time to set up an individual appointment with the school counselor.

❯ Set up a weekly schedule that includes the time your student spends in school and on after-school activities, working, homework, and any other weekly activities. Look at the schedule your student set up in the last step. See all of those blank spaces? Right now, they represent your student's free time. Find two hours to use for college planning.

STEP TWO

CREATE A COLLEGE PLANNING PORTFOLIO

Jasmine was a confident senior who didn't talk very much. When she and her mom came to meet with me for the first time, I noticed that she was carrying a heavy tote bag.

I asked her tons of questions to learn more about her academics and activities, but she replied with one-word answers. It was difficult for me to get a good sense of who she was and what she was passionate about.

Finally, her mother encouraged her to show me the book in her tote bag. It was a huge, three-ring binder that she had decorated with pictures and fun scrapbooking materials. Inside, she had gathered together her academic records, certificates of achievement, and pictures of her favorite activities. As I turned through the pages, I was able to learn much more about her by asking questions tailored to what I was seeing on the pages. Best of all, Jasmine began to smile widely and talk more about herself.

Having evidence of all of her achievements gathered in a single portfolio was a definite confidence booster.

PORTFOLIO

When your student fills out college and scholarship applications, he will be asked many of the same questions about his classes, activities, and goals, over and over again. Collecting all of this information in one place will save your student time and energy.

A portfolio is a collection of personal information, academic records, career goals, and writing samples designed to help your student tell his story when applying for college admission and scholarships. The completed portfolio should reflect not only his accomplishments but also his hopes, dreams, and plans for the future. It is designed to also be an organizational tool so that he has a place to store important items.

Start with a three-ring binder with divider tabs and some page protectors. Then encourage your student to use the steps that follow to create a college planning portfolio that reflects her personality. It should be designed using your student's favorite colors, lots of pictures, and anything else inspiring.

PERSONAL INFORMATION

Your student will need to refer to personal information over and over again while completing applications for jobs, college, and scholarships. Keep it safe, in one place, and protect it well.

- copy of driver's license or state ID

- copy of Social Security card

- immunization record

- income tax returns

- W-2 forms

ACADEMIC RECORDS

Although there are many parts to college applications, academic records are certainly the most important.

One of the first things I ask new students is "What is your grade point average?" I am always surprised at how many students, even college-bound seniors, don't know where they stand academically. Some are not even sure of what a cumulative grade point average is.

A cumulative grade point average is the average of every grade a student has earned since freshman year. It is usually found on the official transcript. If for some reason you can't find it there, you can get in touch with your student's school counseling office.

Your student should also gather college entrance exam scores and graduation test records in this section. We will talk more about the SAT, ACT, and Preliminary Scholastic Aptitude Test (PSAT) in step four.

RESUME

Usually we think of a resume as tool for getting a job, but the college resume serves a slightly different purpose. This one- or two-page document will be your student's quick reference for all of the information needed to apply for summer programs, colleges, and scholarships. Your student may also have occasion to hand this resume to college representatives or other people important to the college admissions process, so make sure it has all of the following sections.

Heading

The top of the college resume will look very much like a traditional work resume and should have these parts: full name, mailing address, e-mail address, and phone number.

If your child primarily uses a nickname, put it in parentheses. For example, my daughter's name is Alexandra, but everyone calls her Alex, so much so that many people don't realize what Alex is short for. In that case, it is important that the nickname is shown.

Please encourage your student to get a professional e-mail address that includes the first and last name. Also, please listen to the voicemail greetings and make sure it is something your student would be comfortable with having a college representative hear.

Education

Your student should list educational accomplishments, which will be requested many times and memorized.

- high school name, address, and phone

- graduation year

- name, phone number, and e-mail address of the school counselor

- specialty program (AP, International Baccalaureate [IB]), Cambridge, performing arts, governor's school)

- special classes (e.g., individual honors classes) and exams

Activities

The things that take up your student's time when she is not in class are important to remember when telling her story. Help her keep records and descriptions of all of her activities since the ninth grade. List the details of her extracurricular activities, work experience, community service, internships, and leadership roles.

The bulk of the information students have to provide on college and scholarship applications is about what they have accomplished during their high school years. Your student should use this section to answer the following questions: What extracurricular activities have you participated in and to what degree? Have you received any honors or awards? Were you an officer in any of your school activities? What have you accomplished outside school?

For now, your student should list everything he has participated in since the ninth grade, along with any offices held, special honors, special projects, and so on. This information can be edited later.

Your student should not only list employment (paid and unpaid) and the position title but also add one-liners describing responsibilities. This is a great time for your student to get assertive in describing the work. Students shouldn't stretch the truth but shouldn't sell themselves short either. "Performed hostess duties" sounds better as "Welcomed guests and escorted them to their seats."

References

Last on the resume, students should list the contact information for at least three references. These can be teachers, coaches, youth workers, supervisors, or any other adult who can vouch for them. They should list as much information (full name, mailing address, phone number, and e-mail) as possible.

You should make sure these individuals consent to being listed as references. You don't want them to be surprised if they get a call about your child. You also want to get a sense of what they might say if asked. If it is anything less than glowing, find someone else.

Skills and Interests

A large part of choosing a college that is the right fit and selecting a good career path is evaluating interests and skills. During the admissions process, students must distinguish themselves from other students. Colleges first look at grades, academic rigor (how hard classes are), class rank, and test scores. These things are important but can be very boring for students to enumerate, and they may, therefore, overlook them.

Under skills, students should list abilities that make them stand out from others—for example, bilingual ability and knowledge of a programming language. They should do the same with interests, listing things that distinguish them from other students.

Accomplishments

Before even considering where to attend college or what the right major would be, students need to get a good sense of what they have accomplished during high school.

There is nothing wrong with students being proud of themselves. This section is where students can be absolutely free to toot their own horn!

- school awards

- National Honor Society membership

- letters of recommendation

- invitations to specialty programs (i.e., governor's school)

- pictures of trophies and medals

- athletic awards

- certificates

CAREER GOALS

Hopefully, by now, your student has given some real thought to possible career paths. Don't worry. She doesn't have to narrow choices down to one choice right away. Help her collect all of her ideas for future careers in this section.

- list of career ideas

- career assessment results

- research on intended careers

WRITING SAMPLES

Having your student's writings gathered in one place can help him avoid starting from scratch each time he applies for a scholarship. This is a great place to keep copies of any personal statements, school essays, research papers, and creative writing. Reuse, repurpose, and recycle those essays! We will talk much more about this in step five.

Pulling together personal information, academic records, accomplishments, writing samples, and more will save time and energy when it is time to start marketing to colleges. It also will give your student a chance to reflect on his accomplishments and begin the college admissions process with a sense of pride.

ACTION STEPS

❯ Gather copies of all of the prior materials into one place. This will be the beginning of your student's portfolio.

❯ Get your student's most recent transcript and answer the following questions together: What is your cumulative grade point average? In which classes have you excelled? Which classes have been problematic? Are you in a specialty program such as advanced placement, Cambridge, or an international baccalaureate? What specialty classes have you taken?

❯ Have your student use the outline at **www.collegemomentum.com/resources** as a guide to creating a resume. Structure and font size is not important. It will be a living document that your student can update as often as needed.

❯ Brainstorm with your student about interests, skills, passions, and talents. The worksheet at **www.collegemomentum.com/resources** is designed to draw out and help students express those unique traits that make them memorable.

STEP THREE

EXPLORE CAREER POSSIBILITIES

Jordyn's mother called me to get advice for her daughter, who she said was interested in becoming a pharmacist. They had done all of the requisite research: where the pharmacy schools were located, how long it would take to complete the education, which schools had accelerated programs, and so on. She said that Jordyn loved chemistry, so a career in pharmacy would be a great fit.

When they came to meet with me, I was surprised. Instead of the very serious future scientist I expected, I saw this attractive, creatively dressed young woman whose bright eyes held my attention immediately. I asked my usual get-to-know-you questions, including "So … tell me why you're interested in pharmacy."

Jordyn's bright eyes immediately went flat, as if I had just asked her to explain the federal tax code. To me, there is nothing more painful than meeting a sixteen-year-old who is not excited about her future. It doesn't take much to excite most teenaged girls, so what was happening here?

As it turns out, she didn't know about very many careers that involved chemistry, nor had she really thought about her other interests when deciding on a career path. She had taken an online career interest survey in which chemist and pharmacist were the only careers that had any relevance for her.

So I took a few minutes to ask her what she was "into." Her personal interests and extracurricular activities centered on art, music, and dance. She and her mother expressed concern that following these pursuits would not make her enough money to live on and that she didn't really have a passion for any one of these things in particular. She simply engaged in these activities as a way to express herself creatively.

At this point I stopped taking notes, looked her square in the eye, and asked her what I call the magic wand question, "If you could wave a magic wand and make it so that all jobs paid the same, what kind of work would you choose?"

Jordyn and her mom looked at each other, lit up like Christmas trees, and started laughing. "She *loves* makeup!" Mom said. They started talking over each other, excitedly, describing how she loved putting makeup on her friends before they went out and how she could spend hours in Sephora. This was her favorite way of expressing her creativity. Nevertheless, she was not interested in a career as a makeup artist. She felt that as a smart young woman with the opportunity to go to college, she should pursue something much more academic, such as chemistry.

Of course, I didn't want her to give up pursuing something related to her passion. I am, however, never going to discourage a student from studying science or math, especially a young woman. But right then, we needed to help her find some ideas that excited her. We brainstormed about some of the things that people with a background in chemistry can do, such as chemical engineering, forensic science, and teaching at university.

Then we hit the jackpot. What if she could use her skills as a chemist to create makeup? She could still wear a white lab coat, but instead of counting pills, she could design new shades and textures of cosmetics. After that revelation, the possibilities were endless. She could work for a paint developer, fabric manufacturer, or art restorer.

As you can see, the process of career exploration is not about eliminating choices but about opening up possibilities.

HOW CAREER PLANNING HAS CHANGED

When many of us started our careers, we expected to work for thirty years in the same general career and retire in our sixties. Things may or may not have worked out that way in reality, but that was considered the ideal.

Our children will be exposed to a completely different career planning process. They are competing on a global scale with a more educated work force. Millennials are also expected to have several careers, some even running concurrently, and they may have several streams of income at once.

Full-time employment may not be the goal for today's students. Instead, part-time work, freelancing, and consulting may be the norm for them. They are more likely to seek situations that allow them to be location independent—work that allows the flexibility of telecommuting from anywhere.[6]

Lastly, and perhaps scariest for older generations, is that today's young people don't expect to fully retire.[7]

---

6 J. Maureen Henderson, "The Young and the Restless: True Tales from the Location-Independent Labor Force," Forbes, March 26, 2013, http://www.forbes.com/sites/jmaureenhenderson/2013/03/26/the-young-and-the-restless-true-tales-from-the-location-independent-labor-force/#75aa2d80715f.

7 "Many millenials expect to work until they die," CNBC, May 31, 2016, http://www.cnbc.com/2016/05/31/many-millennials-expect-to-work-until-they-die.html.

Because they are expected to live to be a hundred or more, they will need to work longer, and they want that work to be meaningful.

PREPARE YOUR STUDENT FOR THE FUTURE JOB MARKET

After sixteen or more years of formal, full-time education, many young people are deathly afraid of the thought of transitioning to full-time work. Can you blame them for being scared?

Many high school graduates (and sometimes even college grads) complete their education without working a single day in their lives. More and more parents are encouraging their children to focus on schoolwork and extracurricular activities to the exclusion of working even five to ten hours per week. As a result, many children don't know what work is like.

In addition, they constantly hear the adults around them complain about their jobs. Why would children look forward to spending their days doing something that many of us are so vocal about hating?

They endlessly get the message that the job outlook is bleak. Despite the fact that unemployment is down overall, we still hear many, many stories about college graduates who have to work in positions that are not ideal because they cannot find work in their intended fields.

Of those college graduates who are qualified for employment, too many are not prepared well enough for the *job hunt*. Colleges offer workshops and seminars on interviewing skills and resume writing, but most do not make this a mandatory part of the curriculum or a requirement for graduation. As a result, far too many students aren't prepared to send out good application packages or meet with recruiters at job fairs.

The good news is that there are ways to put our young people on the right track. It starts with you, the parent. Focus on sharing with your children what you enjoy about working. It may help to make a list of the positives about your work and share it with your children. You may find that you enjoy your work more than you thought or that you're ready for a change. Don't focus on the money because that doesn't mean much to them yet.

Then, encourage your children to work, if only for just a few hours a week. Even jobs such as babysitting and mowing lawns help them understand the value of working for their own money.

Find out the truth about the job outlook. Dig deeper into the job market and discover where entry-level positions are and what they pay. The vast majority of college graduates are able to find positions in their general fields within six months of graduation.

Help your young person take advantage of career readiness resources so that she is well prepared for the job search. Encourage her to use her college's career placement office and to take any career classes offered on campus.

You don't have to wait until your student is in college to start preparing for her entry into the job market. There are programs targeted to high school students such as Future Business Leaders of America (FBLA) and INROADS.

Whether your student is absolutely sure of her career goals or has no idea about where to start, there are some things that you can do to help her head in the right direction.

OCCUPATIONAL OUTLOOK HANDBOOK

One of the best tools for doing some initial research is the *Occupational Outlook Handbook.*[8] This online resource, sponsored by the US Department of Labor, categorizes nearly every job title in the country and gives job descriptions, education required, average salaries, and projected job growth. Even better, your student can see a list of careers related to the one he is exploring.

There are some specific questions that your student can answer using the *Occupational Outlook Handbook.* Is the job he is interested in pursuing a growing field? Will there be jobs available in five years? How much is he likely to be paid?

Check out the Similar Occupations tab (on the specific occupation page) to see all of the related possibilities. For example, many students choose to go into accounting because they like numbers and want to make good money. But how does being an accountant compare to being a financial analyst? Or a mathematician? Who makes the most money? What are the working conditions for each job? You and your student should explore all of the closely related options to learn if he is headed in the right direction.

PROFESSIONAL ORGANIZATIONS

Almost all career fields have professional organizations that represent them. These organizations bring together people in the same career field to share information, set professional standards, and hold conferences.

Many of these organizations also have the mission of bringing more people into their profession, so they often have outreach programs for high school and college students. Joining may give your

---

8   Bureau of Labor Statistics, *Occupational Outlook Handbook*, US Department of Labor, https://www.bls.gov/ooh/.

student access to educational opportunities, networking, internships, and scholarships.

For example, the American Medical Association (AMA) sets standards for the medical profession and advocates on behalf of physicians and patients. Students interested in going on to medical school can also find helpful career planning and scholarship information on the AMA website.[9]

Another use of professional organizations' websites is to discover the cutting-edge professionals who are doing what your student wants to do. If your teenager is not sure what steps he should take, looking at those who are already doing the work in a big way can give him tons of inspiration.

There are rock stars in every professional community. If your student is interested in architecture, for example, she should become familiar with the work of Frank Gehry, who designed the very distinctive Disney Opera House in Los Angeles, and I. M. Pei, who created the glass pyramid entrance to the Louvre in Paris.

While it is not so hard to find the rock stars in careers such as entertainment, architecture, or even astrophysics (Stephen Hawking and Neil deGrasse Tyson come to mind), it can be much more difficult to find rock stars in careers such as nursing, teaching, and accounting. Try looking at the professional organization's websites again to find out who the president is and who is speaking at their conferences.

9   "Becoming a Physician," AMA, https://www.ama-assn.org/education/becoming-physician.

INTERVIEW PROFESSIONALS
IN THE INTENDED FIELD

In my freshman year of college, one of my assignments was to interview a professional in my intended career field. I was majoring in actuarial science, the mathematics behind insurance.

I chose this field because I loved math and knew that there are very few actuaries. I liked the idea of doing something unique and wanted an occupation that would be a little bit different every day. The fact that actuarial science is a highly paid profession was just a bonus.

I was given the contact information for one of the best-known actuaries in the country. I called her office, set an appointment for us to chat on the phone, and prepared a list of questions to ask. I was *very* excited!

I was seventeen and full of brightness and energy, so I was severely disappointed at the lackluster responses I got from her. I asked her what a typical day was like. She talked about sitting in front of her computer for seven or eight hours.

I asked about the project she was working on right then, and her answer was about predictive modeling … something, something … I nearly fell asleep.

The worst answer was to the last question, "What do you love most about your job?" She was quiet for several seconds, thinking. Finally, she said, "The money . . .?"

I promptly changed my major. I knew that there had to be a better option for me.

By the way, several of my college friends have become actuaries and have led happy, successful lives. It just wasn't for me, and I'm glad I discovered that sooner rather than later.

Students don't have to wait until they are already in college to do informational career interviews. If your child has a general idea about the career field she is interested in pursuing, she can start networking with professionals now by conducting informational interviews. Most adults are willing to set aside ten to fifteen minutes to talk with an ambitious young person who is interested in learning more about what they do.

Help your student make a list of people your family knows who work in her chosen career field (or something similar). Think about extended family, neighbors, family friends, and people at your place of worship. Then have her approach one of them to ask for fifteen minutes of their time, either in person or on the phone.

Before the appointment, your student should prepare a list of questions to ask. Help her formulate questions that don't require just a yes or no answer but lead to discussion—questions that elicit interviewees' descriptions of their own passions, interests, and goals. Examples:

- Why did you become a . . .?

- What is a typical day like for you?

- What keeps your passion alive for your career?

- What advice do you have for someone just starting out in your field?

Encourage your student to be on time for the appointment and to spend more time listening than talking or writing. It is very important to follow up with a thank-you note. E-mail is okay, but a personal, handwritten card is much better!

JOB SHADOWING, VOLUNTEERING, AND INTERNSHIPS

Your student should use his time in high school to get hands-on experience in as many fields of interest as possible. The best way to learn about what it is like to be a lawyer, social worker, physical therapist, or anything else, is to spend time with someone who is actually doing that job.

In order to get a deeper understanding of what it takes to be a professional in his chosen career, your teenager needs to spend one-on-one time with someone who has taken that path. Of course, he will not be able to try cases in an unpaid internship at a small law office, but he will see firsthand what the day-to-day life of a lawyer entails. He will also have the invaluable opportunity to be guided through his career by a mentor.

When I first met Alison, for example, she wanted to become a physical therapist. She had a general idea about what physical therapists did, but she wasn't sure how much time she would have to spend in school or how much money she could reasonably expect to make.

After doing her research, Alison realized that the educational commitment of seven years to become a physical therapist was much more than she wanted to give. In addition, she was volunteering at a hospital three days a week during the summer, which made her realize she wasn't interested in working in a hospital at all. She decided to become a massage therapist and work while she earned a business degree. Her ultimate goal became opening her own business and managing other massage therapists.

If your student is still undecided about her career direction, this is not the time to add pressure. Just have her choose something she finds interesting and research that. This is just a jumping off point, and you will work together to help her narrow down the possibilities.

ACTION STEPS

⊗ Advise your student to use the *Occupational Outlook Handbook* to answer the following questions:

   ▸ How much is the entry-level salary for this position?

   ▸ What education do I need to get started in this career?

   ▸ What are the best schools?

   ▸ What is the future job outlook?

   ▸ What are three professional organizations that I can join?

   ▸ Who are the power players in this profession?

⊗ You and your student should find some professional organizations that serve her intended career. Help her choose one to join and become an active participant.

⊗ Brainstorm with her places where she could find job shadowing opportunities and start contacting them.

STEP FOUR

FIND "RIGHT FIT" COLLEGE MATCHES

Noah had always dreamed of attending a large university. He had gone to a small K-12 private school with less than 350 students and was very active in his small church. For college, he longed to be surrounded by lots of people from various backgrounds. He wanted to get lost in the crowds at football games and share experiences with students that were not like him.

He visited a dozen large colleges with his family. His father wanted him to go to a major Catholic school such as the University of Notre Dame and Georgetown University, while his mother favored top-tier public universities, such as the University of Virginia and Penn State.

After spending a busy visitation weekend at his top-choice college, Noah realized that navigating four years at a school of fifteen thousand or more students might not be the right fit after all. He convinced his parents to let him visit a couple of small Catholic colleges with enrollments of three thousand or less and immediately felt more comfortable. His parents could see the difference in how he interacted with the students and staff at the smaller institutions.

Despite his initial desire to go to a very large campus, Noah's research led him to find the right fit in a small, cozy college.

GET SPECIFIC ON WHAT YOU'RE LOOKING FOR IN A COLLEGE

At the end of the junior year, students are busy with testing and finishing up projects for the year. Even so, college applications are looming, and getting a good list of potential colleges early on will help to ease the process. Starting to compile a list of potential colleges before the end of the junior year makes the process less stressful in the fall of the senior year and prevents students from throwing together a haphazard list of schools that may or may not be a good fit.

YOUR STUDENT'S QUALIFICATIONS

Before getting her heart set on any one college, your student should go back through her portfolio to evaluate her own grades, test scores, activities, goals, and accomplishments. This self-evaluation will help her be critical about matching herself to colleges that will accept her.

Campus Culture

Students should get the feel of the campus by asking questions such as:

- Does the college have students who are like me?
- Does it have groups that represent my interests?
- Do I see myself living here for the next four years?

Students should take amenities such as extracurricular activities and religious affiliation into consideration, but they should also be flexible when considering these things.

When it comes to extracurricular activities, students should not be discouraged if the college does not have every desired club or activity. Students don't have to participate in formal groups to find others who share their interests. If a club doesn't already exist, students can form their own.

Distance from Home

Many students dream about going to college as far away from home as possible. However, the reality is that the majority of students attend college within a hundred miles of home.[10]

Academic Programs

Students and parents often decide against a college that may be a great fit because it doesn't have a specific major. Although there are some career paths that require a particular undergraduate major, in most cases, students can be creative and select a major close to what they're looking for. They can then choose electives that are specific to their vocational interests.

Corey, for example, was absolutely sure that he wanted to be an FBI agent. He was convinced that he had to major in criminal justice. He was frustrated to find that some of the colleges he was most interested in did not have a criminal justice program, but many offered criminology or forensic science. We chose five of his top colleges, and, from each, we looked at the major that most closely resembled criminal justice. We printed out each curriculum to compare them side-by-side. Corey was surprised at the similarities and the differences. As it turned out, the curriculum that mostly resembled the training he was looking for was called justice studies, but he found ways to add electives to several criminal justice and criminology programs that he felt offered the

---

10   Krista Mattern and Jeff N. Wyatt, "Student Choice of College: How Far Do Students Go for an Education?" *Journal of College Admission*, 203 (Spring 2009): 18–29, https://eric.ed.gov/?id=EJ838811.

training he was seeking. Ultimately, he chose to attend a program in criminology in the Washington, DC, area.

Career Support Options

Since most of us and our children attend college primarily for vocational training, we want to make sure that the chosen school will actively assist in preparing our child for the workplace.

Cost of Attendance

Steps six and seven are dedicated to the discussion of this topic.

HOW COLLEGES EVALUATE STUDENTS

Now that your student has given some serious thought to what would make a college a good fit, the next step is to look at how colleges decide what students will be a good fit for them. Every college will have specific admissions criteria that are unique to their needs. However, most traditional four-year universities evaluate students using some basic, common measures.

Academics

Colleges evaluate students academically using two criteria: academic rigor and grades. Academic rigor refers to the difficulty of the classes taken in high school. It comes as a surprise to many students that this is the first thing that colleges evaluate on the transcript. For most colleges, this is as important as the actual grades earned.

Students should take the toughest classes they can handle while maintaining their target GPA. This is a balancing act and may require course correction every semester.

Cumulative Grade Point Average

Colleges will see every semester or yearly grade that your student has earned since the ninth grade. This also includes any high school credits earned in middle school (such as foreign language or algebra credits).

To account for varying academic rigor between high schools, colleges will often unweight a student's grades before comparing them to students from other school districts. Unweighting means recalculating any grades that were originally weighed on a 5.0 scale back to the traditional 4.0 scale.

Test Scores

Most four-year universities require a standardized entrance exam (SAT or ACT) as part of the admissions package. Despite their differences, they are used interchangeably by virtually all traditional colleges.

Students and parents need to devise a strategy about when to take the tests and whether to take one or both exams. A common plan (and one that I endorse for most students) is to fit study time for each test into the fall of the junior year and plan to take both tests in the early spring. That way, the student has an opportunity to choose the test that is the best fit and study before taking the test one more time in the fall.

However, some colleges are implementing a test-optional policy that allows students with high grades to submit the application without ACT or SAT scores.

I am often asked, "Shouldn't my student just take the test as many times as it takes to get the highest score possible?" Higher is always better, but more can be detrimental. Taking the tests too many times can look desperate and opens up the possibility of declining scores. A sample strategy could be to take the SAT in March and the ACT in April of the junior year and spend the summer studying for the best one to retake in early fall.

It helps that most colleges use a process called superscoring, which involves taking a student's highest score for each section on the SAT, even across separate test dates.

Every Saturday and every dollar is precious, so encourage your student to spend time every week doing something that will help move him forward on the test. I suggest that your student set aside part of the two or more hours of college planning time for structured test preparation, starting eight to twelve weeks before the first scheduled test and continuing until he has taken the last one. In addition, your student should plan to spend ten minutes practicing on the other six days. Students can sign up for the SAT question of the day, have practice questions delivered to their phone, or watch instructional SAT videos on KhanAcademy.org. ACT also has practice questions and tests at ACT.org.

For weekly practice, work with your student to come up with a structured plan. This can range from working through a test preparation book on his own to participating in a classroom or online class to hiring a tutor to come to your home. There are advantages and disadvantages to each method, so choose what works best for your student's study style.

Many universities also require or highly suggest that applicants take one or more SAT subject tests. The subject tests allow students to demonstrate their proficiency in a specific academic area not covered on the general SAT, such as French, world history, or chemistry. Work with your student to develop a plan to fit the SAT subject tests into the overall testing strategy.

Activities

Colleges are interested in knowing what your student does when not in class. Their purpose is not to see how much she can fit into her schedule but to learn what she is passionate about. On the resume that we discussed in step two, your student should list extracurricular activities, sports, community service, and work experience in order of importance to her. It is okay to leave out activities that she did not participate in for very long or that do not contribute to the story she is telling.

You often hear that colleges are looking for well-rounded students, but that is not quite accurate. They are actually looking for a well-rounded student body. A college can admit one student who excels in music and another student who excels in athletics, so it doesn't need one student to do both. Your child doesn't want to show he is the student who does everything. Help him show, instead, that he excelled at those things he is passionate about and let go of anything that doesn't move him.

When I met with John, he told me about the activities he participated in. I could tell immediately what he was passionate about as opposed to what he did simply because he thought he should. He was very engaged in sports but wasn't enthusiastic at all about doing random volunteer work and some of the music activities that he participated in. We worked together to craft his applications to highlight his participation and accomplishments in cross-country skiing, soccer, and lacrosse and to show how he developed athletic and leadership skills.

Essay/Personal Statement

The essay, or personal statement, is the only part of the written application where your student gets to show some personality and really set herself apart from the next student. Encourage your student to spend some time thinking about the story she wants to tell.

We will discuss essays and personal statements in depth in step five.

Letters of Recommendation

Many colleges will require applicants to submit one or more letters of recommendation as part of the admissions process. The purpose is to help the admissions team learn more about the student than what grades and test scores can tell. Students should think, early on, about which adults they will ask to lend support to their college applications.

Each college specifies how many letters of support they require (or highly recommend). They will also detail from whom those letters should come—usually counselors and teachers. Letters can also come from other adults who know the students well, such as coaches, supervisors, scout leaders, or youth pastors. Recommenders should be people who have known the student for a year or more and can speak to the student's best qualities.

It may seem natural to choose teachers of subjects in which the student excels. However, the teachers of subjects students have struggled with and in which they have improved their performance might be able to give more insight into personality traits the admissions panel is interested in learning about.

Even though the school may require students to use its online system to request letters, students should also ask for their recommendations in person. If someone they ask seems less than enthusiastic, they should find another recommender. A bland, dispassionate letter can be worse than no letter at all.

Your student should give the recommenders all of the materials they need to complete the letter quickly and easily. This includes a resume outlining the student's achievements. If the recommendation must be completed using a paper form or needs to be mailed in, your student should be sure to provide those items along with a stamped, addressed envelope.

After everything has been submitted, remind your student to thank recommenders. E-mails are okay, but handwritten notes are much more personal and memorable. Your son or daughter may need their help again, so they should go above and beyond to express gratitude. This thoughtfulness will certainly be remembered.

Additional Criteria

Some colleges or programs may require or encourage interviews with admissions staff or alumni, portfolios from prospective art or fashion students, music or drama auditions, or creative extras such as videos.

FINDING OUT IF YOUR STUDENT AND THE COLLEGE ARE RIGHT FOR EACH OTHER

Now that your student has made a list and learned more about what each college is looking for, it is time to narrow down to the few that will be a good fit. The best way to learn more is to interact with college representatives as often as possible through visits, college fairs, and information sessions.

College Visits

No matter what your student's year is in high school, college visits should be part of your plan. It is essential before choosing a university that you visit several campuses of different sizes and types. Families often visit schools that are similar to one another, but that is a mistake. Early in your student's college search, seriously consider visiting schools that vary in size, setting (such as urban versus rural), and specialty (liberal arts versus research). That small private college that wasn't even on your radar may surprise you, or you may discover that the Big Ten university has a more intimate feel than you anticipated.

One of the most pleasantly surprising college visits that I have made as a college counselor was to Hampden-Sydney College, a private men's college in Virginia. The young men that I met there were among the most focused and engaging I had met on any college campus. I immediately thought that a few of my students who were not even considering an all-male environment should see it. One of them visited and applied there and to several other small private institutions. Ultimately, he attended a different small college and was extremely pleased with the result. He received enough scholarship money to make the out-of-pocket cost equivalent to that of the large public university he had initially considered.

Another fantastic counselor tour I experienced was at Lake Erie College, a tiny liberal arts college in Ohio. Almost every college student we walked past smiled and spoke to us. A few even stopped to tell us why students should consider going there. We ate lunch in the dining hall and learned that the university president ate there with the students every day. He talked with us for about ten minutes before inviting over another professor to spend the rest of the time eating with us. We got so much more out of this visit than we would have by sticking to the usual go-to-an-information-session-and-walk-around-campus visit.

Almost all colleges will show you the basics on their daily tours—main classroom buildings, the library, dining hall, a dorm—but these things tend not to be the major points of differentiation for most students. I absolutely urge you to do traditional college visits, but here are some activities you can add to give you a deeper sense of what each school is really like.

Sit In on Actual Classes

Students spend a lot of time in class, so they need to know what that experience will be like. They should ask to sit in on a typical freshman class such as composition 101 or psychology because these are the first classes they will take. Is the class taught by a professor or a teaching assistant? Are there fifteen students or five hundred?

Students may also ask to visit an upper-level class in their intended major, but they should remember that it may be a couple of years before they are able to take this type of class.

Hang Out in the Library

Colleges love to talk about the volume of resources in their campus libraries, but visitors should try to not be overly impressed with that. They should look for the number of students using the library as a study space and seeing if the librarians are actively helping students. They should also find out if there are lots of study groups.

Talk to Current Students

Your campus tour guide is trained to answer all of the questions you may have, so please ask away. However, there will be thousands of other students on campus on the day of your visit. Listen to what students are talking about as they walk through campus or eat at the dining hall. Don't be shy about connecting with a few of them. Ask what they like best about the school or what they would change.

On a visit to Virginia Tech, as our bus pulled up to the main campus, several students started cheering and yelling, "Come to Tech!" Even after we left the bus and they realized we were counselors and not prospective students, they took the time to talk with us about why we should recommend Virginia Tech to our students. This left us with a clear sense of the energy and excitement that Hokies have for their school.

Visit on a Friday

I'm not a big fan of making a Saturday open house your first visit to a college, because you're not getting a real feel for what the school is like on a typical day. I do, however, love going on a Friday. Classes are still in session, but students are getting geared up for the weekend.

On Friday, you can get a better sense of what students are doing while in relaxation mode. Are there groups of students gathering in the yard to play intramural sports? Is there an impromptu concert happening near the fine arts building? Or are most students coming out of their rooms with bags so they can head home for the weekend? You'll get a very clear picture of the weekday and weekend culture of the campus if you visit on a Friday.

Sleep in the Dorm

The absolutely best way to learn about a campus is to stay there for a day or two. By connecting with a current student through the admissions office or through a friend, your teenager can visit overnight, during the week, and do everything with that student: go to class, eat in the dining hall, and hang out with the student's friends. This will give your child a clear sense of the tiny details that can't be seen on a general college tour, including whether the bathrooms are clean!

You can set up your college tour online through the admissions office, but do not hesitate to ask for help in adding more to your visit.

College Fairs

High schools, churches, and other community groups invite college representatives to set up information tables so that prospective students and parents can learn more. Typically, students attend a college fair with the idea of visiting as many tables as possible to collect brochures, T-shirts, and other swag. Most of this stuff just ends up in the trash, and the students don't have any more information than they did before the night began.

Instead, students should attend college fairs with a plan and have a list of colleges they intend to visit, mapping out where to find them at the fair when they get there. They should also bring several copies of their resume and a page of labels with their name, school, address, phone number, and e-mail printed on them. This will make it much easier to provide information to colleges instead of having to write it out each time.

The people staffing the tables at most college fairs are admissions officers, who are likely to be key in making admissions decisions. The students' goal in speaking with these representatives—especially when students are seniors—is to get them to remember them at decision time.

Students become memorable by identifying themselves as already knowledgeable about their school and asking thoughtful questions. They shouldn't ask about things that are easily found on the college's website. Instead, they should inquire about things specific to their own situations.

Here are some examples:

Major

- How many students from your college go on to medical school (or law school, etc.)?

- What types of internship do students in my major tend to get?

- Are there research opportunities with faculty?

Admissions

- What are the benefits of being in the honors program?

- What are the advantages of applying early?

Campus Life

- What percentage of students live on campus after the first year?

- What is unique about your campus community?

Financial Aid and Scholarships

- How many freshmen receive merit-based scholarships?

- Does your school consider a student's need for financial aid when making admissions decisions?

The college representatives may not know the answers to all of your student's questions, so your student should follow up with an e-mail the next day. This will help him to be remembered for all of the right reasons at decision time.

High School Visits

During college fair seasons (fall and early spring) admissions representatives will set up visits to local high schools, especially at ones that have had many students apply in previous years. Students absolutely must attend these visits because they will have an opportunity to learn even more specific admissions information firsthand.

Just as at college fairs, the admissions representative hosting the information session is likely to be the gatekeeper regarding applications from that high school. Also, the more interaction students have with their admissions representatives, the more favorably colleges look at them.

Encourage your student to attend the visit with his resume and a couple of very pointed, well-thought-out questions. Again, the student should not ask anything that can be easily found on the college website. Instead, questions should give the college representative insight into why that student would be a good fit.

Creating a list of right-fit colleges involves knowing what

TIP:

If your student is shy about talking to the college representatives, he can practice by talking with representatives from those colleges that don't already have a line at their tables. These schools often are just starting to recruit students in your area or are simply overlooked by the crowd. If your student is willing to talk to them, he may find that they are looking for a student like him. Even if that's not the case, at least he will get some practice chatting with college representatives to prepare him for the next step. ⚑

the student wants, what the parents can agree to, and what the colleges are looking for. It will take research, visits, and talking with other families to get a good feel for what is right for your family.

In the next step, we will explore how to let colleges know they are a good fit by writing a powerful personal statement.

ACTION STEPS

❯ Use any of the online search engines to start researching an initial list of colleges. You and your student are likely to come up with dozens. Considering too many colleges is not helpful, because the details start to get hazy. Instead, help your student make a list of ten to fifteen potential colleges that meet her criteria. Talk about what all of these schools have in common and what makes them favorites. This will not be the student's final list but rather a living document to be updated as your student changes her mind about potential colleges.

❯ Start arranging college tours at the top choices as soon as possible. It is never too early to visit, and you can plan to visit several times if necessary. Put any college fairs, open houses, or high school visits on the family calendar.

❯ Identify upcoming college fairs in your community and make plans to attend one or two. You can find a comprehensive list at the National Association of College Admissions Counselors website.

STEP FIVE

CRAFT A POWERFUL
PERSONAL STATEMENT

Anya was an excellent student. She had high grades, strong SAT scores, and a well-rounded resume. She had put together a good list of right-fit schools that were known for their engineering programs.

We had been working together for several months, and she did everything I assigned her to do quickly and efficiently. Nevertheless, I noticed she was hesitant to work on the essay. As many students do, she found the idea of writing about herself to be daunting, and she was having trouble coming up with ideas.

We ended up having a really fun brainstorming session. I asked her questions about her unique interests, her greatest accomplishments, and what she thought made her different from her classmates. She started telling me stories about her family, and that was when I felt I was seeing the real Anya for the first time.

Anya had been adopted from China by an American family. Her new mom was a single lawyer who was also caring for her own parents, who were from India. Anya's home life was a rich cultural tapestry of American, Indian, and Chinese culture. She realized that her story would make her memorable for all the right reasons.

Anya used her story to respond to an application prompt that asks students to tell something meaningful about their background. She decided to share the story of her adoption.

She spent a couple of weeks brainstorming, drafting, revising, and proofreading to get to her final, polished essay. Once that first essay was uploaded to her application, she turned her attention to the other essays that she had to write for admissions and scholarships. She now felt much more confident about the process of writing the next few personal statements, so these were written much faster.

Best of all, Anya was able to use the first essay over and over again. Three of the colleges on her final list had not seen her essay on her cultural background. When another application prompted her to include an image of a significant place and share the story, Anya submitted a picture of the region where she was born and a slightly shorter version of the essay on her cultural background. And when she needed to write a three-hundred-word essay about someone with whom she would love to have dinner, she chose her birth parents— essay number three.

In total, Anya revised and reused this essay five times during her senior year alone. She saved herself hours of valuable time by choosing a great story that gave insight into who she was and that she could tell over and over again.

INTRODUCTION

Most four-year colleges will require or highly recommend applicants to submit at least one writing sample, and typically, they call this the personal statement. Colleges use the personal statement as a way to learn more about students' personalities.

This is the part of the process where so many students get stuck. The rest of the application is rather cut and dried. They have to answer questions about where they live, where they go to school, what activities they participate in, and what their grade point average is. But the personal statement is where students get to show a little bit of personality and tell the admissions panel who they are on the inside. Of course, the essay is judged on whether or not the students can write well, but it is first evaluated on whether or not the students give a little piece of themselves and describe what makes them different from other students. So, instead of being afraid, students should think of the personal statement as an opportunity to shine, be creative, and say a little bit more about who they are.

The essay will be evaluated on mechanics and content, but none of that matters if it isn't interesting and memorable. Students should not just repeat the activities and accomplishments that were listed in the first part of the application. Also, this is not a term paper. Instead of treating it as if it were a school assignment, help your student to think of the personal statement as an opportunity to write creatively and reveal personality.

In the same way the rest of the application process can be completed, the essay can be completed using the proven step-by-step method that I will outline in the next few pages. The good news is that students already know how to do this. They have written plenty of essays throughout high school, and this is just another one.

TOPICS

Before they begin to think about what to write, it is a good idea for students to become familiar with the types of prompt that colleges use to get essays. Some prompts are very specific, but many are open and extremely vague. For example: *Give us a personal statement of five hundred words.* This prompt gives almost no direction at all. If your student is faced with such a prompt and has no idea where to begin, he can use one of the following prompts as a jumping-off point.

QUESTIONS FROM THE COMMON APPLICATION

The Common Application is a form that can be used to apply to several colleges at once. Students using the Common Application are required to respond to one of the following prompts with an essay of up to 650 words.

- Some students have a background, identity, interest, or talent that is so meaningful they believe their application would be incomplete without it. If this sounds like you, then please share your story.

- The lessons we take from obstacles we encounter can be fundamental to later success. Recount a time when you faced a *challenge, setback, or failure.* How did it affect you, and what did you learn from the experience?

- Reflect on a time when you questioned or challenged a belief or idea. What prompted your thinking? What *was* the outcome?

- Describe a problem you've solved or a problem you'd like to solve. It can be an intellectual challenge, a research query, an ethical dilemma—anything that is of personal importance, no matter the scale. Explain its significance to you and what steps you took or could take to identify a solution.

- Discuss an accomplishment, event, or realization that sparked a period of personal growth and a new understanding of yourself or others.

- Describe a topic, idea, or concept you find so engaging that it makes you lose all track of time. Why does it captivate you? What or who do you turn to when you want to learn more?

- Share an essay on any topic of your choice. It can be one you've already written, one that responds to a different prompt, or one of your own design.

EXAMPLES OF UNIVERSITY QUESTIONS

- What work of art, music, science, mathematics, or literature has surprised, unsettled, or challenged you, and in what way? (University of Virginia, College of Arts and Sciences)

- Students are often told what classes they should take. If you had the opportunity to create a class, what would it be and why? (Georgia Tech)

- What makes you happy? (Tufts University)

- There are twenty-seven amendments to the US Constitution. What should be the twenty-eighth? (University of North Carolina at Chapel Hill)

- Tell us about spiders. (University of Richmond)

As you can see, the essay topics can vary widely. The exciting part is that they present an opportunity for students to display their creativity and originality. Since students will most likely have to write several essays, they can use the following steps to create the most engaging stories possible.

BRAINSTORMING

After students become familiar with the essay prompts from their chosen colleges, or the Common Application, the next step is to choose one prompt that can be answered by one of their stories. Instead of choosing the prompt and then finding a story to match, students should first develop a list of the stories that best reflect what they want the admissions officers to know about them.

Students can start by asking themselves a few questions.

- What is my story?

- What are the things that make me different?

- What should I tell an admissions representative whom I am meeting for the first time and who knows nothing about my grades and activities?

- What one story from my life would give a stranger a better sense of what makes me tick?

They should list incidents from their lives that are interesting, funny, sad, or inspirational. At this point, this list doesn't have to be very long or detailed.

Some examples:

- why I started the anti-bullying club at my school

- the trip to New Orleans I took with my school marching band

- the time I went on a laundry strike at home and it backfired

- what I learned from having to change my life because of celiac disease

Students should be able to come up with five to ten ideas they can write about. If they are having trouble, this is a great time for them to start consulting with members of their dream team (created in step one). These people can help by sharing their own stories about your student.

WRITING THE FIRST DRAFT

Now that your student has chosen the story he wants to tell, he can focus on quickly writing out a first draft. The goal is to simply get the main points scripted out. This is not the time to focus on grammar or sentence structure. This step is just about creatively telling the story from beginning to end.

When writing this first draft, students should keep in mind the emotion they want to evoke. They want to leave the reader with a feeling, not just with information but with a connection. After reading hundreds or thousands of applications, admissions representatives will need a reason to keep reading the entire essay and remember the student. Students should add as many details as possible to make the reader feel they are right there sharing the experience.

── TIP: ──

For inspiration, have your student Google the words "essays that worked." What comes back is a list of colleges that post their favorite essays from previous years. None of them are typical, and few are written in the five-paragraph style (introduction, three body paragraphs, conclusion). These personal statements can be used as examples of what colleges are looking for. Your student shouldn't try to emulate the work these students did but simply read these essays for inspiration. ⚑

Encourage your student to write this first draft in one sitting. She does not need to worry about adding the introduction or conclusion. She should just tell the story.

The personal statement is not an opportunity to restate the resume and list every achievement. Students should not write what they think the college representatives want to hear.

REVISING AND REFINING

Revising the essay involves making sure that the story reads well and sounds as if it were written in the student's voice. Your student should use the following checklist to make the necessary revisions and refinements.

Rubric/Checklist

- ○ Answer the question asked.
- ○ Open with a compelling first line.
- ○ Show your personality by giving some insight but not too much.
- ○ Create a connection with the reader.
- ○ Describe how you will be a good fit for the school (not by using the sentence "I will be a good fit because . . .).
- ○ When you read it out loud, does it sound like your voice?
- ○ Does it make you want to read it to the end?
- ○ Does it show off your personality?

- O Does it elicit a feeling or emotion such as pride, empathy, laughter, and so on?

- O Does the essay flow easily from beginning to end?

- O Is it told in the first person (using "I")?

- O Does the story make a point?

TIP:

Reuse, recycle, repurpose. As Anya (from the beginning of this chapter) was able to do, your student will also be able to use this essay again and again. It will be extremely useful for your student to have two or three stories that can just be dusted off and repurposed throughout the college application process and when applying for scholarships.

An important part of college admissions success comes from the engaging stories students are able to tell about themselves. This step becomes much easier when it is approached in a creative, yet systematic, way. 🚩

EDITING

The last step is editing for grammar and punctuation errors and typos. The essay should be edited again and again. Students should then have somebody else look it over, put it away for a day or two if they have that kind of time, and come back to it with fresh eyes so they can see mistakes. This is the only part of the essay creation process where students can strive for near perfection.

Students certainly do not want to send off something that has a glaring error in it. They may get away with one misplaced comma, but it is hard for the reader to look highly upon an essay that appears never to have been spell-checked. So you should let editing be your student's very last step and it should be done several times over.

ACTION STEPS

❯ Brainstorm, as a family, to find interesting stories your student can tell.

❯ Offer to assist by giving feedback based on the provided checklist. Remember to use the sandwich method: positive comment, constructive criticism, positive comment. Students are often very sensitive about the writing process, so offering encouragement is crucial.

STEP SIX

BEAT THE COST OF COLLEGE

Luis and his family came to the United States from Colombia when he was in the ninth grade. Within two years, Luis learned English and became one of the top students in his high school class. He especially excelled in math and science, and his goal was to become a chemical engineer. Unfortunately, Luis's father was in the USA on a work visa, so Luis was considered an international student and could not qualify for in-state tuition or federal financial aid. The family depended on scholarships to pay for college expenses.

I met with Luis and his parents for the first time in December of his senior year. He was very interested in attending a large state school with a strong engineering program, such as Virginia Tech, Georgia Tech, or the University of Michigan. With a 4.3 grade point average and nearly perfect SAT scores, finding scholarship money shouldn't have been a problem, right?

Wrong.

By waiting until December to get started on the application and scholarship process, Luis missed out on most of the large community, corporate, and college-based scholarships that students with his profile compete for. In fact, I placed several calls to engineering schools to help Luis find scholarship money. One dean was clearly disappointed that Luis had waited so long.

"We had several scholarships available for students like him. We just awarded a full scholarship to another international student entering our chemical engineering program, but his application wasn't as strong. We would have awarded Luis the money if he had applied ten days ago."

Luis and his family were absolutely devastated. After reevaluating his options, the Luis decided to live at home and attend a community college for two years before transferring to a four-year university. This saved his family tens of thousands of dollars in tuition and living expenses.

Luis excelled in community college just as he had in high school. He was able to complete his bachelor's degree with a full-tuition scholarship at a top engineering school. Although Luis's college experience did not begin as he had hoped, he found another way to achieve his goal of becoming an engineer.

THE COST OF ATTENDANCE

One of the hardest parts of college planning is taking a realistic look at the cost of college. You will find a range of $4,000 to $5,000 a year for community college to more than $70,000, including expenses, for the most expensive schools.

When comparing colleges to each other, you want to be sure that you are using the yearly cost of attendance as your measurement, especially if your student will be living on campus. Looking only at tuition rates does not give the full picture of what it will really cost to attend that particular school.

In addition to tuition and housing, cost of attendance includes estimates for books, supplies, travel to and from campus, computer, dormitory expenses from sheets to shower shoes, interview clothes, and more. Some students may also need to purchase athletic equipment or special supplies such as nursing scrubs or engineering software. Out-of-pocket expenses can total a few thousand dollars, especially in the first year and right before graduation.

To help determine the cost of each college on your student's list, search each college website for the net price calculator. It gives an estimate of the total cost of attendance including tuition, room and board, and other expenses. This will almost never be your out-of-pocket cost. Merely use this as a starting point.

You will find vast differences in cost even within one geographic area or type of college. Even colleges within the same state university system may vary widely in cost because of different campus resources or the cost of living in their locations.

CREATING A PLAN

As we discussed earlier in step one, coming together regularly as a family to discuss college plans is crucial, and that includes having several sessions regarding money. Everyone in the family, including the student, should be on the same page about how college will be paid for.

Discuss the resources available, savings, other assets, and assistance from your extended family. Determine how much your family has available for all four years—no judgment, just the truth. Communicate this reality to your student ASAP.

Young people are often confused about money in part because parents shelter them from the realities of it. They have no idea what it takes to support the family because parents hide it from them. Therefore, they think that everything is great and their parents have all the money they need to go to any college they desire.

This is a great time to stop insulating your children from the financial realities of college costs and what paying for college means for you. Will you have to work for five more years? Equate that with their having to spend five more years in high school. Will you have to pay for college with loans? Show them how many hours they will have to work at their part-time jobs to earn the loan payment.

The average college graduate has over $30,000 worth of student debt that has to be paid off over the next ten years. That is a lot for a twenty-two-year-old to handle. The goal of this section is to provide options to make the best long-term plan for paying as much college expenses as possible before borrowing funds. Loans should be the last resort to pay for college.

Once you know how to leverage your financial resources and those from outside your family, you will be in a better position to ensure that your child is not saddled with more debt than she can handle.

"I'm sure she'll get financial aid" is not a plan. Neither is "he can pay for it himself." If you can't just make $25,000 appear from thin air, how can you expect your seventeen-year-old to do it?

You wouldn't spend this kind of money on a home or a car without evaluating how it would affect your finances overall. You can try to learn all of the ins and outs of financial planning or you can work with someone experienced.

Remember that college is a six-figure investment. It is worth a few bucks to save money through online tax saving, retirement protection, and so on. Treat this as the major investment that it is.

TWO STRATEGIES

It will take a combination of strategies to keep the amount of loans to a minimum. There are two major categories of strategy: lowering the cost of college and finding additional resources.

Lowering the Cost

The first step to paying less for college is bringing the cost down as low as possible.

College-Based Scholarships

The most direct way to pay for college is to get college-based scholarships. Virtually every university has full and partial four-year scholarships for both incoming freshman and upper-classmen. When students are in the admissions process, they should make certain that they are also applying for every dollar of scholarship money offered by the college. We will talk more about this in the next step.

Community Colleges

Families can defray the cost of college by using a local resource: the community college. Many states have guaranteed admissions programs that allow students to start taking classes at community college with the plan to transfer to a four-year college later. One of the reasons that this is so popular is it saves families around $40,000.

Another way to save thousands of dollars is by taking classes at the local community college during the summer. Instead of staying at their base colleges all year, students who are falling behind in their credits or are working to get out of school a semester early can take general courses at the community college for a fraction of the cost and avoid paying room and board for those extra months.

Free Colleges

For high-achieving students who are already considering a career in the military, one of the five US military service academies may be an attractive option. The US Military Academy (West Point), the US Air Force Academy, the US Naval Academy, the US Coast Guard Academy, and the US Merchant Marine Academy do not charge for tuition, room, and board in exchange for several years of active-duty military service upon graduation. The admissions process at the service academies is extremely competitive, so students should not wait until the senior year to start planning.

In addition to the service academies, there are other colleges that offer students alternative ways to pay for their tuition and housing. One strong example is Berea College, a small liberal-arts school in Kentucky. Every student who is accepted to Berea College receives a full scholarship. In exchange, students work on campus for fifteen to twenty hours per week. Berea is just one of seven federally recognized "work colleges."

Off-Campus Housing

In some communities, especially small college towns, it may be cheaper for your student to live off campus. Be careful because sometimes there are hidden fees that come with having to live off campus, such as having a twelve-month lease instead of a nine-month lease. There are other considerations, such as safety and the expense of traveling to the campus. However, if you do the math and you see that it is much less expensive for the student to live off campus, that can save you a lot of money too.

Finding More Resources

Now that you have worked to reduce your costs as much as possible, you can start looking for ways to bring in more money to pay down the bill.

Budget Adjustments

The first way to make the difference is to do your own budget adjustments. The years before you have a child headed off to college are a great time to meet with a financial planner who is an expert at finding the leaks in your monthly budget. Saving $500 per month without drastically changing your lifestyle can save your family from having to borrow $24,000 during your student's college years. You may be surprised at how much you can save by lowering your cable bill or eating out less often.

A few years ago, Myra and her daughter Tiffany came in for some financial aid advice. Tiffany was a senior and had done very well in high school, and Myra was extremely concerned that they were not going to be able to afford college. They were very surprised and disappointed that, based on their family income, they probably weren't going to qualify for any federal Pell Grants or other need-based aid. Later that afternoon, I happened to bump into them at the drug store. We chatted outside the store for a moment, and I watched, dumbfounded, as they got into their brand new, fully loaded, luxury SUV. All I could do was shake my head. They were driving away in a vehicle worth three years of college expenses.

Federal and State Grants

Grants are a form of financial aid that does not have to be paid back. Most grants are need based, meaning that eligibility is based on a family's finances. The largest federal grant program is the Pell Grant, which is awarded to students who demonstrate considerable financial need.

Although grants may not be a reality for many middle-income families, the only way to find out is to apply using the Federal Application for Federal Student Aid (FAFSA). Also, many state-based grants are less income focused. For example, the Virginia Tuition Assistance Grant is a non-need-based grant for Virginia residents attending a private institution in the state. Check with your intended colleges and your state council on higher education for more information on state grants for your student.

Extended Family

Grandma and grandpa may love to shower their grandchildren with nice gifts. However, at the point when you are planning to pay for college, perhaps cash would be more useful. Ask grandparents, aunts, uncles, and godparents to put some money in the student's college savings plan. Pull on their heartstrings a little by telling them that you sure hope that little Johnny doesn't have to graduate under a mountain of student debt.

Employee Benefits

Many employers have tuition reimbursement programs or small scholarship programs for staff. Sometimes, they are not well advertised, so talk to someone in your human resources department to find out what is available. Additionally, many employers offer 529 college savings plans that allow you to contribute directly from your paycheck.

Tax Benefits

There are several tax credits and deductions that your family may be able to take advantage of during your student's college years.

These include the American opportunity tax credit, lifetime learning credit, and deductions for tuition, fees, and student loan interest. Talk to your tax preparer about how these benefits apply to you.

Veteran's Benefits

As a parent, you can transfer your GI Bill and some other veteran's benefits to your children. Please make sure that you start working with your VA administrator early to apply the benefits in the way that maximizes them for your student.

Student Contribution

Students who work and earn $200 per month can avoid borrowing almost $10,000 during the four years of college. Earning some money toward college will help them learn to budget. It will also give them some skin in the game by making their own financial contribution to their education. There is also the fact that you are not spending all of this money to teach your child to be a college student. Your goal is to help your child learn to become a working adult. Learning to work, save money, budget, and build a resume is part of the process.

Federal Work-Study

Federal Work-Study is a federal financial aid program that allows students to earn money for college by working on campus a few hours per week.

Work-study jobs are designed to allow students time to get schoolwork done. Some of the best for that are at the library or the recreation center, where the entire job may simply be to watch students swipe in and out.

When I was in school, I was a math major and worked for one of my professors. I filled out a few forms, picked up library books, and helped students with calculus. Most days, though, I spent my work hours studying. The best part is that Dr. Donaldson was right there if I had a question about my own work.

Service Commitments

Students can earn money toward college by taking a gap year and serving with a service organization such as AmeriCorps. AmeriCorps volunteers serve in locations across the country, and at the end of their service they get a stipend that they can use toward college expenses.

Another example of a service commitment is the Reserve Officers' Training Corps (ROTC). In exchange for a four-year military commitment, students earn scholarship money. They also receive training for one weekend a month and two weeks per summer to enter the military as an officer.

Paid Internships

Internships are important for helping students learn about their intended careers and make connections with professionals who can help them in the future. Although many internships are unpaid or only pay enough to cover room and board for the duration, students who plan early can find internships that also pay a salary. Set the expectation early that your student will seek paid internships during his summers.

I met Maya when she was finishing her sophomore year at New York University (NYU). She and her parents already had $60,000 in student debt, and she still had not decided on a major. Her parents were at wit's end because she didn't understand how devastating that amount of debt was. They were hoping that having someone else talk to her would be helpful.

On our first Skype call, I found out that Maya was planning to stay in New York that summer to take one class and do an unpaid internship. That meant her parents were shelling out $7,000 in tuition, rent, and expenses for that three-month period, and she wasn't earning a dollar in return.

I challenged her to go back to the internship office at NYU and find a paid internship. The internship staff there matched her with a small nonprofit organization that she wasn't thrilled about at all, at first, but it paid $250 a week and gave her time to take her class.

When I spoke with her a couple of weeks later, she was very excited. She had met someone she was looking up to as a mentor, and she felt much more confident about settling on a major. She was mostly excited that she had earned some money to send back to her parents. Just having a couple of talks and the importance of being able to contribute made all the difference for her.

Skilled Self-Employment

Your student probably already has skills that can earn him money at a college, maybe without even having to venture off campus. For example, students with strong academics can work for agencies that are looking for college students to tutor elementary, middle, and high school students. They can earn up to $35 an hour or more, especially if they are proficient in math, science, writing, or certain foreign languages.

One of my students, Callie, was interested in personal training. She loved working out and found herself coaching her friends when they were at the gym together. She started the process of getting certified as a personal trainer while she was still in high school. When she was accepted to college the next year, she worked out a deal with the recreation department that allowed her to teach fitness classes in her dormitory and charge a small fee at the door. She found a fun way to follow her passion and make some extra money.

Resident Assistants

For students who are people oriented and like living in the dorm, becoming a resident assistant (RA) can be a great way to cut college costs. RAs help to run the dorms, settle arguments between roommates, and make sure everybody is following the rules. In exchange, they get free room and board, which can be as much as half of all college costs.

Loans

You can see that the common theme throughout this section is that you should avoid borrowing if at all possible. Almost all sources of funds are better than borrowed money. Taking out too much in loans will delay your student from being able to buy a car, purchase a home, or move out of yours.

Borrowing too much could also keep you from retiring, paying off your home mortgage, or supporting your own aging parents. Before borrowing, consider whether or not it is worth sacrificing these things ten, twenty, or thirty years into the future.

If you have exhausted all other resources and have to borrow, shop around. Check the current federal student loan rates and terms at studentaid.gov. Most families will first consider federal Direct Loans and federal PLUS Loans.

Federal Direct Loans (also referred to as Stafford loans) are borrowed without the need of a cosigner or credit check. Students can borrow up to $31,000 total over the course of their undergraduate education and have ten years after graduation (or dropping out) to repay. The advantage of federal Direct Loans is that they have a relatively low interest rate and many fail-safes to help students avoid default.

Parents can borrow on behalf of their children using federal PLUS loans. There is a credit check with PLUS. However, it can be used to borrow the entire cost of attendance. Parents also have ten years to repay, but that time period begins immediately. Also, the PLUS has significantly higher interest rates and origination fees.

Compare the federal rates and terms from banks, credit unions, and other lenders. Many families also consider borrowing against their own assets, such as their homes, retirement plans, or whole-life insurance policies. *As with any other major financial decision, please meet with your financial and tax advisors to discuss the long-term ramifications.*

Negotiation

Your last strategy, once you have received financial aid offers from the schools where your student has been accepted, is to negotiate with each college for more gift aid. This strategy does not work with every school, but you may be able to get small private colleges to work with you. This is particularly effective if your financial situation has changed within the last year or if you have received an attractive offer from a different college.

Gathering the financial resources to pay for college is like putting together a puzzle. It requires time, patience, and creativity. It also requires that your student participate both by earning money to help and by doing what we will cover in step seven: finding scholarship resources.

ACTION STEPS

❯ Go to the tuition and financial aid pages of your student's prospective colleges and find the cost-of-attendance information. Note the similarities and differences based on the type of college and location.

❯ Sit down, as a family, and figure out how much you have available for college expenses.

❯ Go through your monthly budget and decide where it makes sense to make some budget changes.

STEP SEVEN

MAKE IT RAIN SCHOLARSHIP DOLLARS

When I met Derek, he was a first semester senior with a 4.1 average in a very challenging advanced placement program. His SAT scores were quite solid but not exceptional. Derek was also an outstanding soccer player, but he was not interested in playing on a college team, just intramurals.

I met with Derek and his mother on a Saturday morning during the fall of his senior year. Derek prepared for his meeting with "the college lady" by printing out his resume and putting on a suit and tie. He greeted me by looking me in the eye and giving me a firm handshake.

Derek clearly articulated his dream of attending Duke University to study accounting. We discussed how the family finances would affect his choice of college. Derek's father had passed away a few years earlier and had left some money for him and his sister to attend college. Unfortunately, the family did not have quite enough to pay out of pocket for a private university such as Duke.

I worked with Derek to create his final list of colleges. It included a variety of private schools and public colleges. We also added two "safety" schools, where not only was he almost sure to get in, but he would probably be in the top 10 percent of applicants.

Derek was admitted to most of the colleges to which he had applied, including Duke. He also received several scholarships from other colleges, but he did not get a lucrative offer to attend the school of his dreams and become a Blue Devil. He still could have gone to Duke, but it would have meant taking on about $50,000 worth of loans over the four years. Derek, ultimately, decided that although Duke was his dream school, he would attend the college that offered him a full scholarship so that he could graduate debt-free.

I met up with Derek's mother again, five years later. This time, we were going through the college admissions process with her daughter. Of course, I asked about Derek to find out how things had worked out for him. She was over the moon about Derek's success. She excitedly told me that while Derek was in college, he was able to take a semester in South Africa, and he spent one summer doing an internship in London. He used some of the money that he did not need to spend on tuition to pay for his plane tickets and out-of-pocket living expenses while abroad.

After graduation, Derek moved to New York to work for a large Manhattan firm. He also proposed to his college sweetheart and started making plans for the wedding. Derek's mother was even more excited about Derek's upcoming wedding because of the gift that she was able to give him and his fiancée: the down payment on their New York apartment.

For Derek, passing up his first college and choosing the one that was willing to pay him to attend allowed him to take advantage of some amazing opportunities and graduate without debt.

WHY SCHOLARSHIPS ARE IMPORTANT

Despite all of the news stories we hear about how expensive college has become or how student loan debt has affected young college graduates, many of the students from middle-income families I work with believe their parents have enough money to pay for college out of pocket. They believe that finding scholarships is not that important and will be a waste of time.

So why is it really important to find scholarships?

Scholarship money can make the difference between a student going to college where she *wants* to go and going where she *has* to go. More expensive colleges become more affordable. Also, scholarship money can be used to free up funds for other important educational experiences such as study-abroad programs or graduate school. Students can list renewable or prestigious scholarships on their resumes as proof of their resourcefulness.

No matter what your family's financial situation may be, it makes more sense to get someone else to pay for your child's education. The more money that comes from outside resources, the more money your family will have left over for other things. Most importantly, scholarship money will reduce the amount that your family will have to borrow. Lower loan payments (or none at all) mean that young people can start off their postcollege life without the burden of loan payments.

TYPES OF SCHOLARSHIPS

Scholarships come from a variety of sources, including corporations, nonprofit organizations, and the colleges themselves.

College-Based scholarships

Have you ever heard of a graduating senior who has won $300,000 or more in scholarships?

Students who achieve this major feat have usually won full four-year scholarships from several universities. They are not going to be able to use all of that money, since they can only attend one university at a time, but isn't that a problem that you would like your student to have?

Students should always look for scholarship money from the schools to which they are already planning to apply. These awards can come in many forms from different sources on campus.

Renewable Four-Year

Every university offers a limited number of four-year scholarships for incoming freshmen. They are often called presidential or trustee scholarships. These highly coveted awards frequently require students to apply for admission earlier than most students or fill out an additional application form. Be warned that these scholarships are very exclusive and are reserved for the very top students.

Example: The University of Notre Dame offers about sixty-five merit-based scholarships for incoming freshmen. This represents about 3 percent of enrolled first-year students.

Automatic Scholarships

Many colleges automatically offer scholarship awards to students who meet certain benchmarks for grade-point average and test scores. Automatic scholarships are usually found at private universities, but there are a few public colleges that offer them as well.

Example: At Virginia Wesleyan University in Virginia Beach, all admitted students are considered for freshman scholarships based on their high school grades and SAT or ACT scores. Using Virginia Wesleyan's scholarship calculator, a student with a GPA of 3.6 and a *composite score of 27 on the ACT can expect $24,000 in institutional scholarships.*

Departmental Scholarships

Individual academic departments within a university may offer its own scholarships for freshmen. Check the home pages for your intended academic department and major for criteria and application instructions.

Example: *Virginia Tech in Blacksburg, Virginia, allows students to search for awards by logging into the Scholarships Gateway on its website. Students can find information for awards from the College of Architecture and Urban Studies, College of Engineering, Department of Music, and more.*

Scholarships for Out-of-State Students

Very often, the difference between attending a public college in your own state and one in a different state comes down to price. A part of your tax dollars is allocated to supporting public institutions in your state, and, in return, you get a discounted rate on the tuition. You do not get this discount when your student attends a public school in a state where you do not have residency.

If your student is looking at out-of-state colleges anyway, look to see if they have scholarships, grants, or discounts that are specifically for out-of-state students. If your student is determined to go out of state, take steps to bring the price down so that you're not paying a premium for him to do so.

Example: *Ohio State University has the National Buckeye Scholarship for non-Ohio residents. So if you are a resident of a* *different state and you decide to go to Ohio State, you can get up to $12,000 per year (the amount quoted in 2016) knocked off tuition, and that may bring your cost down to the same level as the cost of your own state university.*

Scholarships for International Students

Students at US universities who are not citizens or permanent residents of the USA may not only be ineligible for federal financial aid but also may have to pay expensive international rates at public and private colleges. Many schools that wish to make themselves more attractive to international students offer special scholarships to make tuition more affordable to those students.

Example: American University in Washington, DC, offers scholarships for international students that range from $6,000 to $25,000. They are renewable for all four years of study and are only available at the time of admission.

Corporate Scholarships

Many of the places where we shop and eat set up foundations that award scholarships and other support to current and future high school students. Corporations do this not only because it puts their brand out front but also because it supports the communities where their customers live. Large companies often offer hundreds of scholarships per year. However, there is usually rigorous competition for these national awards.

Examples: The Coca-Cola Scholars Foundation awards almost $3.5 million in scholarships every year. The Gates Millennium

Scholars Program, established by Microsoft cofounder Bill Gates and his wife, Melinda, provides scholarships for outstanding minority students with financial needs.

Career-Based Scholarships

In step three, we discussed exploring professional organizations for career information, but they can often have scholarships as well.

Example: *Let's say that your student is interested in becoming an engineer. There are a number of professional organizations to look into. The American Society for Engineering Education and the American Nuclear Society both have scholarships for incoming freshmen. Students of color can check the list of scholarships from the National Society of Black Engineers. The Society of Women Engineers has resources for female students who are studying science and engineering.*

Reserve Officers' Training Corps (ROTC) Scholarships

If your student is interested in joining the military after college, ROTC scholarships can help defray the cost. In return, participants commit to serving eight years with the military.

Example: *The ROTC Program is available at over 1,100 colleges and universities nationwide.*

Personal Interests

Not all scholarships are academically based. Students with special interests such as fashion design or camping can often find scholarships that are more focused on those skills than on their grades.

There are scholarships for bowling, rock climbing, and even making your prom outfit out of duct tape.

Example: *The Gamers in Real Life (GIRL) Scholarship is open to all students interested in a career in video game design, and female gamers are highly encouraged to apply. The winner is awarded $10,000 and an internship with Daybreak Games in San Diego.*

Community-Based Scholarships

The last overlooked group of scholarships is local or community-based scholarships. Scholarships sponsored by local businesses or community groups tend to be smaller and are often not listed on the big scholarship engines such as Collegeboard.org, Fastweb.com, or Scholarships.com.

Many young people leave this money on the table because they feel that filling out applications for a $500 or $1,000 scholarship is not a valuable use of their time. When I talk to young people about making the effort, I ask them how long it would take them to earn $500 at their after-school job. When comparing that to the time it takes to fill out a few applications, they can usually see that finding scholarships is worth the effort.

To learn more about community-based scholarships, make sure that your student is keeping in touch with the school counselor. The counselor will be able to advise your student about how the school distributes scholarship information, such as in a weekly bulletin, files in the career center, or through an online resource such as Family Connection.

Example: *Local Optimist International clubs sponsor the Optimist Oratorical Contest and the Optimist Essay Contest. Once students* *win at the local level, they compete at the district level, where the first prize is $2,500.*

I share this with you because people think there is some magic bullet for winning scholarships. The truth is that it is only done with elbow grease. Students only win scholarships they apply for.

ACTION STEPS

- ❯ Find out from your student's counselor where scholarship information is curated. Make sure the counselor knows that your son or daughter is serious about doing the work.

- ❯ During your student's weekly college planning time, identify one scholarship application to complete.

- ❯ Make sure your student reads through the entire application and has everything to complete it, including the essay if needed. If your student does not have an appropriate essay already written, help her prioritize to use the first hour to write and refine. Once the essay is complete, complete the other parts of the application before sending it. *Do not end the planning session until this is done.*

- ❯ Make sure your student has contacted anyone who has agreed to write a letter of reference. The reference will need your student's resume prior to writing the letter.

STEP EIGHT

PUT IT ALL TOGETHER

Chloe was a self-proclaimed procrastinator. Despite being a good student, she put off everything for as long as possible and was often late with her school assignments. Chloe's mother, concerned that Chloe would miss out on getting into the colleges of her choice because of her habit of missing deadlines, enlisted me to mentor her through the college application process.

Together, Chloe and I reverse-engineered her application process knowing that she would be inclined to do things at the last minute. We used a spreadsheet to create a timeline that included every step, especially application deadlines and scholarship due dates.

Despite all of this detailed planning, Chloe was having difficulty hitting her targets in the first couple of weeks. We realized that the spreadsheet was not visual enough for her. She decided to use a colorful wall calendar to plot out her weekly tasks for school and for college planning. That made all the difference. Now Chloe could visualize when items were due and she was more inclined to get them done. In addition, her mom could help to keep Chloe accountable by just pointing to items on the calendar.

With her master wall calendar, Chloe was able to develop the new habit of planning early and meeting her deadlines with ease.

THE APPLICATION PROCESS

The previous seven steps in this book were laid out so that this last step would be (nearly) painless. Students who failed to plan early find the application process to be frustrating because they try to make all decisions at once instead of making crucial choices over a period of several months. They also often complete their applications during their extremely busy fall semester. Your student, however, has a different plan to follow. Completing the applications should feel like just another step and should not cause more anxiety.

As I stressed in step one, organization is key to warding off anxiety. Start with a spreadsheet to organize this step. Your student can create one or download the one that I created at www.collegemomentumacademy.com/resources. Your student should also have the portfolio handy throughout this process.

Your student may also want to plot out the big steps on a wall calendar or in a planner. It is helpful to break the entire admissions process down into weekly goals and block off time to work on them.

For example, a weekly goal may be to commit four hours to completing the first personal statement. The daily tasks may look like this:

Monday: brainstorm and outline.

Tuesday: write the rough draft.

Wednesday: revise and refine.

Thursday: complete final edits.

Your student can then plug that one hour per day into her calendar for that week. Committing to particular times to get the work done is crucial to staying on track.

THE SUMMER BEFORE THE SENIOR YEAR

The summer is a key time to get as much done as possible while classes are not in session. I strongly advise setting aside at least one hour per day to accomplish the following tasks.

Complete the Final List of Colleges

Narrow down the list to the final five to seven colleges.

Use the spreadsheet at www.collegemomentumacademy.com/resources to list selected colleges with application deadlines and requirements.

Study for the SAT or ACT

Your student should use the summer for test preparation if he is planning to take the SAT or ACT again in the fall. He can use a free resource such as Khan Academy (www.khanacademy.org/sat), or you can enroll him in a course. Private tutoring is also a great option for students who need a boost in a specific test area.

Write the Essays

Taking the time to write the personal statements and essays before doing the applications will eliminate the desire to push them off until the last minute. Your student will then be able to put the time into this very important (and often frustrating) part of the process that it needs and deserves.

Complete Applications

Although applications will not be due until fall, most forms will be available during the summer. August is the perfect time to start completing the basic information needed on each form.

Your student should begin with knowing which applications he will be completing. Many universities have their own specific applications. Over seven hundred universities, however, now use the Common Application (www.commonapp.org), which allows students to apply to several colleges at once. Many colleges also use the Universal Application (www.universalcollegeapp.com) or the new Coalition Application (www.coalitionforcollegeaccess.org). Your student can find out which application is appropriate by visiting each college's admissions website.

Absolutely the best plan for your student is to work consistently through all of the applications within one week. He should not consider this step finished until he has completed all of the parts of the application that he can do himself, including uploading the essays if required. The letters of recommendation and transcripts will be added later.

Auditions, Art Portfolios, and Interviews

Programs in the visual and performing arts, architecture, and interior design usually require students to audition or submit portfolios of their work. For example, students applying to the Corcoran School of the Arts and Design at George Washington University must submit their portfolio of ten to fifteen pieces using SlideRoom, their online portal. In addition, the school hosts a National Portfolio day at which faculty members will offer feedback on students' work. Your student should check with his intended colleges in August to find out when to submit work.

Students who have applied for specialty programs, such as honors or leadership, may be required or encouraged to participate in an interview. Use this time in late summer to plan out that activity and learn when it can be scheduled. It is extremely helpful once the student has learned the name of the interviewer to research that person on Facebook and LinkedIn to learn more about him or her.

SEPTEMBER/OCTOBER

The fall semester of the senior year is already extremely hectic without the pressure of college applications. Since your student has already completed most of the difficult parts of this process, she can remain focused on schoolwork, extracurricular activities, and finding scholarship resources.

Request Transcripts

Follow your student's high school rules about requesting transcripts. Counseling offices may require that your student submit transcript requests ten to fifteen days before they are due, so those dates should be placed on the master calendar.

Once the first request is submitted, there is usually no need to ask for midyear grades to be sent. They will be sent automatically, and the final transcripts will be sent once the final college choice has been made.

Letters of Recommendation

Your student can ask for letters of recommendation from all counselors and teachers well ahead of the due date. For recommenders who are not from the school (coaches, youth pastors, scout leaders), your student should also provide a resume and a note detailing the reasons for asking for their help and directions for submission.

Apply for Scholarships

As we discussed in depth in step seven, the fall of the senior year is prime time for students to dive into the scholarship process.

The application deadlines for larger scholarships tend to be in the fall. Plan to use that two hours of college planning time to apply for scholarship money every week.

Apply for Financial Aid

As we discussed in step six, October is the time to apply for grants, loans, and work-study using the Free Application for Federal Student Aid (FAFSA.ed.gov). Some families will also need to complete an additional form called the College Scholarship Service / Financial Aid PROFILE (css.collegeboard.org).

You may be nervous about the process if this is your first time completing financial forms for your children. It goes much easier if you have the right documents in front of you when you begin. Use the following list to make sure you have everything you need before you start the FAFSA.

1. Full names, birth dates, and Social Security numbers for the student and parent(s).

2. An FSA ID for the student and one parent (visit fafsa. gov if you do not already have one).

3. Alien registration number for the student if applicable.

4. List of potential colleges.

5. For parents, the date of the most recent marital event (marriage, remarriage, separation, divorce, or widowhood). You will not need to do this if you are single.

6. Your most recent tax forms and W-2 forms. You will be able to upload tax information directly from the IRS, but it is helpful to have those documents on hand.

7.   The amounts in your checking, savings, and investment accounts. This does not include retirement accounts or the value of the primary home. For more details, see the FAFSA page "What Is the Net Worth of Your Investments?"[11]

8.   The amount that your student earned from working.

9.   The amounts in any student-owned checking or savings accounts.

Remember that the FAFSA is a student-based form, meaning that all questions are directed at the student. This also means there is an expectation the student will participate in completing the form. This is a great opportunity to let your son or daughter engage in the financial aid process, even if it is just by helping you type.

Many colleges would like to have a clearer picture of the family finances than the FAFSA is able to offer. The CSS Profile gives colleges the opportunity to learn more about your income, assets, and expenses. It takes longer than the FAFSA to complete and will require you to have available information regarding your primary home, rental property, retirement accounts, and more. There is also a fee to complete the profile.

The advantage of completing the profile is that the colleges that ask for this form are typically qualifying students for additional scholarship and grant funding. It takes a little more time, but it is worth it to avoid leaving money on the table.

---

11   "What is the net worth of your investments?" FAFSA, https://fafsa.ed.gov/fotw1617/help/fotw33c.htm.

NOVEMBER THROUGH JANUARY

If your student has been following this plan, all of his applications should be submitted by the end of October. So now what? There are plenty of important steps your student can take while waiting for letters of acceptance.

Follow Up on Applications

Your student should use this time to follow up on each application to be sure the university has received everything. This can usually be done by logging back into the application itself. Act on any items on your to-do list.

Show Appreciation for Those Who Helped

Encourage your student to send thank-you notes to his counselor, teachers, coaches, and anyone else who assisted him in the application process. E-mails are okay, but thoughtful, handwritten notes are truly special. I have kept every single personal card I have received over the years, and the young people that took the time to send them stand out in my memory just a little more.

—— **TIP:** ——

Do not call or e-mail the admissions offices to check on your student's application. Your student can do this himself online. It does not reflect well on him for his parents to reach out unnecessarily on his behalf. If you must reach out on an issue that your student cannot resolve without assistance, have him make the call or send an e-mail from his own account.

FEBRUARY THROUGH MAY

Encourage your student to enjoy the last few months of high school while staying focused on his studies. The colleges to which he applied will continue to get his grades through graduation. They will also receive reports on any adverse behavior. Colleges can rescind admissions decisions if students party too hard or have a sharp decline in grades.

Your student should definitely continue the search for scholarships through the end of the school year. There will still be many opportunities in the spring. He should really have the hang of it by now, and many of the scholarship applications he finds now may be simpler and more straightforward than many of those he found earlier in the year.

TIME TO CHOOSE

If all has gone well, your student has gotten acceptance letters from several colleges, and it is time to make a decision about which one to choose. If no college clearly stands out, go back to your family's guiding principles for direction.

Remember Derek from step seven? He chose to take the offer from the college that offered the most scholarship money because of his family's guiding principle of avoiding loans. Noah from step four decided to attend the small college where he felt most comfortable. His family was ultimately more concerned that he attended a school with the right culture rather than more prestige.

If it comes down to the final two colleges, and your student just cannot seem to make a decision, visit the schools again. Take advantage of admitted students days, overnights, or even just the walk-on tours. Talk to current students, both during your visits and on student review websites such as Unigo.com. Consider where your student's friends are going, and encourage her to do the opposite. College is supposed to be a new experience, not a replay of high school.

Once your student has made her final decision about which college she will attend in the fall, your family will need to send a deposit to hold her spot. Most universities set a deposit deadline of May 1, but it may be earlier for special programs. You may also need to send the deposit earlier to reserve a dorm room if campus living space is limited.

KEEP SAVING MONEY

No matter how much your student received in scholarships and financial aid or what your family has saved, it will be extremely helpful to save a little more. Create a plan for your student to save part of his earnings from his summer job for spending money during his freshman year.

Don't let him go crazy on "senior stuff." It is easy to spend thousands of dollars on senior pictures, class rings, spring break trips, and prom. It seems so important at the time, but do you still wear your high school class ring? Help him remember that high school graduation will still be an important highlight of his life no matter how much he spends.

FINAL THOUGHTS

My desire for all families is for their students to have a fulfilling, productive, and safe college experience that sets them up for career success and financial independence.

This success begins when the goal is clearly in focus and the incremental steps to that goal are clearly laid out. Parental support and guidance are crucial for students to make the best decisions. They also need parents who can help keep them calm by staying calm and level-headed themselves.

The earlier families begin taking action on career planning, portfolio building, college exploration, and saving for college expenses, the less overwhelmed their students will be during senior year.

The best outcome is not a result of finding the perfect school or perfect major but of finding the right type of college and a major that starts students off in the right direction.

Students are more likely to feel confident about choosing a college and major when they have done hands-on investigations into their possible career choices. Help your student get as much exposure as possible and find mentors to guide the way.

There are many ways—especially through scholarships—to defray the cost of college. Finding money takes work, and every dollar your family can find beforehand will save money, interest payments, and stress later.

Keep calm, follow the steps, and stick to your family's guiding principles. You and your student can do this—together.

ABOUT THE AUTHOR

Felice Douglas, founder of College Momentum Academy, is a college and career strategist and financial aid expert with nearly twenty years of experience encouraging students to reach their educational goals. Felice is deeply committed to improving the lives of youth from all backgrounds through access to education. Her presentations are lively, engaging, and filled with useful, relevant information.

Through her workshops, coaching programs, and writing, Felice shows college-bound students exactly how to complete the college application process with less stress during the transition from high school to college.

The consistent feedback from hundreds of students and parents is that Felice has a unique ability to take confusing information and break it into easy steps, providing reassurance to her clients.

RESOURCES

For the latest information and access to our upcoming events, visit and like our Facebook page at **www.facebook.com/collegemomentumacademy** and follow us on Twitter at **@collegemomentum**.

CAREER INFORMATION

Occupational Outlook Handbook (OOH): www.bls.gov/ooh

The OOH can help you find career information on duties, education and training, pay, and outlook for hundreds of occupations.

American Medical Association: www.ama-assn.org/

The AMA is an example of a professional organization that provides career information for future practitioners.

LinkedIn: www.linkedin.com

LinkedIn is a social network for professionals. Students can use it to connect with professionals in their intended fields.

COLLEGE FAIRS

National Association for College Admissions Counseling (NACAC) College Fairs: www.nacacfairs.org/

Search NACAC's list of college fairs to find one in your area. The site also lists specialized fairs, such as those for performing arts and STEM.

COLLEGE ENTRANCE EXAM PREP

ACT: www.act.org

Students can get information about preparing for and registering for the test.

SAT: https://collegereadiness.collegeboard.org/

This site has a variety of resources about the test, including how to register for the SAT Subject Tests.

Khan Academy: https://www.khanacademy.org/test-prep/sat

The College Board and Khan Academy have partnered up to provide free SAT practice tests and videos.

ESSAYS/PERSONAL STATEMENTS

"Essays that worked"

Search this term online. You will get a list of links to several colleges, such as Johns Hopkins University, Connecticut College, and Tufts University, that publish example essays.

PAYING FOR COLLEGE

Military Colleges and Academies: www.usa.gov/military-colleges

Learn about military schools and service academies, which train future officers, doctors, engineers, and professionals.

Work Colleges Consortium: www.workcolleges.org/

Seven distinctive liberal arts colleges promoting useful integration of Work-Learning-Service.

Federal Student Aid Information: www.studentaid.gov

Read about the types of financial aid available from the government and other sources.

Free Application for Federal Student Aid (FAFSA): www.fafsa.gov

The application for federal grants, loans, and work-study.

CSS/Financial Aid PROFILE: https://student.collegeboard.org/css-financial-aid-profile

The application for nonfederal financial aid from almost four hundred colleges, universities, professional schools, and scholarship programs.

529 College Savings Plans: http://money.usnews.com/529s

A list of 529 Plans by state and information about how to choose the best plan for your family.

SCHOLARSHIPS

College Board: https://bigfuture. collegeboard.org/scholarship-search

Find scholarships, other financial aid, and internships from more than 2,200 programs.

FastWeb: www.fastweb.com

Access to over 1.5 million scholarships to help you pay for college.

Scholly: https://myscholly.com/

Scholarship platform that helps students find scholarships that match their skills and needs.

University of Notre Dame Merit-Based Scholarships: https://meritscholarships. nd.edu/scholarships/

Virginia Wesleyan College Scholarship Calculator: www.vwc.edu/admissions/ financial-aid/scholarship-calculator.php

Virginia Tech Academic Scholarships: http:// finaid.vt.edu/undergraduate/typesofaid/ scholarships/academic-scholarships.html

The Ohio State University Merit-Based Scholarships: http://undergrad.osu.edu/ cost-and-aid/merit-based-scholarships

American University Scholarships International Students: http://www.american.edu/ocl/

isss/Financial-Aid-and-Scholarships-
for-International-Students.cfm

**Coca-Cola Scholars:
www.coca-colascholarsfoundation.org/**
The Coca-Cola Scholars Foundation invests in exceptional high
school students who are dedicated to leadership, service, and
action that positively affects others.

RESOURCES FOR ENGINEERING STUDENTS

**American Society for Engineering
Education: www.asee.org**

American Nuclear Society: www.ans.org

**National Society of Black
Engineers: www.nsbe.org**

**Society of Women Engineers:
www.societyofwomenengineers.swe.org**

**AmeriCorps:
www.nationalservice.gov/programs/americorps**
AmeriCorps is a domestic community-service program that
allows students to earn money for college.

**Reserve Officers, Training Corps:
http://todaysmilitary.com/training/rotc**
In exchange for money toward education, cadets commit to serve
in the military after graduation.

Gamers in Real Life: www.daybreakgames.com/home

Offers a $10,000 scholarship for students interested in careers in gaming.

Optimist International: www.optimist. org/e/visitor/scholarships.cfm

Local Optimist International clubs sponsor scholarships for the winners of their essay and oratorical contests.

COLLEGE APPLICATIONS

Many universities use centralized applications that allow students to apply to several colleges at once.

The Common Application: www.commonapp.org

The Universal Application: www.universalcollegeapp.com

The Coalition Application: www.coalitionforcollegeaccess.org

GW Corcoran School of the Arts and Design application process: https://undergraduate.admissions.gwu. edu/freshman-application-process

ADDITIONAL RESOURCES

**Resources for Military Families:
https://studentaid.ed.gov/sa/types/
grants-scholarships/military**
This page provides helpful links for information for the GI Bill, Veteran Affairs (VA) Education Benefits, special loan programs, and scholarships specifically for the families of military personnel.

***How to Raise an Adult: Break Free of the Overparenting Trap and Prepare Your Kid for Success* by Julie Lythcott-Haims**
Lythcott-Haims, the former Dean of Freshmen at Stanford University, offers real-world advice about overhelping our children, especially through the college admissions process.

For direct links to all of these resources and more, visit College Momentum Academy at www.collegemomentumacademy.com/resources.

FELICE DOUGLAS

IS FOUNDER OF COLLEGE MOMENTUM ACADEMY, WHICH OFFERS:

- ⊙ individual coaching and mentoring for students preparing for the college admissions process

- ⊙ workshops for middle and high school students and their parents

- ⊙ online courses on essay writing, finding scholarships, and more

- ⊙ summer camps for students looking to get a jump on finding the right-fit college

www.**COLLEGEMOMENTUMACADEMY**.com

CONTACT:
PO Box 6758
Woodbridge, VA 22195
703.680.4780
888.978.5726 toll free
felice@collegemomentumacademy.com

Printed in the USA
CPSIA information can be obtained
at www.ICGtesting.com
JSHW012041140824
68134JS00033B/3185